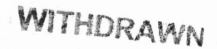

ROCK
AND
HAWK

ALSO BY ROBINSON JEFFERS

What Odd Expedients

The Last Conservative

The Double Axe

The Woman at Point Sur

The Alpine Christ and Other Poems

Poetry, Gongorism and a Thousand Years

Cawdor and Medea

Flagons and Apples

Selected Poems

Beginning and End and Other Poems

Selected Poetry

ABOUT THE AUTHOR

ROBINSON JEFFERS was born in Pittsburgh, Pennsylvania, in January 1887. The son of a minister and professor of theology, he was taught Greek, Latin, and Hebrew as a boy and studied in Germany and Switzerland before entering the University of Western Pennsylvania (now Pittsburgh) at fifteen. He continued his education on the West Coast after his parents moved there, and received a B.A. from Occidental College at age eighteen. His interest in forestry, medicine, and general science led him to pursue his studies at the University of Southern California and the University of Zurich. He married Una Call Kuster in 1913, and in 1914 the couple moved to Carmel, California, where they raised twin sons and lived quietly in a house by the sea for the rest of their lives. In a long and controversial poetic career, he published over a dozen volumes of verse, including *Tamar*, *Roan Stallion*, and *The Women at Point Sur*, as well as a translation and adaptation of Euripides' *Medea*, which enjoyed a considerable theatrical success when it was produced in 1947. A final book of verse, *The Beginning and the End*, was published after his death at the age of seventy-five in January 1962.

ROBERT HASS is the author of *Field Guide* and *Praise*. A collection of his essays, *Twentieth Century Pleasures*, received the National Book Critics Circle Award in criticism in 1985. He lives in Berkeley, California.

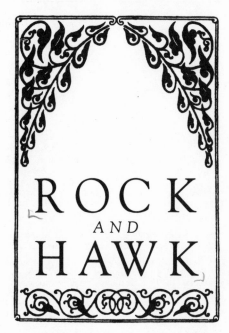

ROCK
AND
HAWK

A SELECTION OF
SHORTER POEMS BY
ROBINSON
JEFFERS

EDITED BY ROBERT HASS

RANDOM HOUSE   NEW YORK

TO WILLIAM EVERSON

Most of the poems in this work were previously published in the following
collections published by Random House, Inc.:

The Selected Poetry of Robinson Jeffers. Copyright 1938 and renewed
1966 by Donnan Jeffers and Garth Jeffers.
The Beginning and the End and Other Poems by Robinson Jeffers.
Copyright © 1963 by Donnan Jeffers and Garth Jeffers.
Selected Poems by Robinson Jeffers. Copyright © 1965 by Donnan Jeffers
and Garth Jeffers. Reprinted by permission of Random House, Inc.

Grateful acknowledgment is made to Liveright Publishing Corporation
for permission to reprint previously published material:

"The Humanist's Tragedy," from *Dear Judas and Other Poems* by Robinson
Jeffers. Copyright © 1977 by Liveright Publishing Corporation.
Copyright 1929 by R. Jeffers. Copyright © 1957 by Robinson Jeffers.
Poetry from *The Double Axe and Other Poems* by Robinson Jeffers.
Copyright © 1977 by Liveright Publishing Corporation. Copyright 1948
by Robinson Jeffers. Copyright © 1975 by Donnan Call Jeffers and
Garth Jeffers. "Prelude," from *The Women at Point Sur and Other Poems*
by Robinson Jeffers. Copyright © 1977 by Liveright Publishing
Corporation. Copyright 1927 by R. Jeffers. Copyright © 1955 by
Robinson Jeffers. Reprinted by permission of Liveright Publishing
Corporation

Library of Congress Cataloging-in-Publication Data
Jeffers, Robinson, 1887–1962.
Rock and hawk: A selection of shorter poems by Robinson Jeffers.
I. Hass, Robert. II. Title.
PS3519.E27A6 1987 811'.52 87-9612
ISBN 0-394-55769-7

Manufactured in the United States of America
24689753

BOOK DESIGN BY LILLY LANGOTSKY

CONTENTS

INTRODUCTION

Robinson and Una Jeffers first saw Carmel Bay in the fall of 1914. It must have been in that year as beautiful as any place on earth. A rocky coast, ridges of cypress and pine, ghostly in the fog. On clear days the Carmel River glittered past the ruin of an old Franciscan mission, and the surf was an intense sapphire, foaming to turquoise as it crested. Gulls, cormorants and pelicans among the rocks, hawks hovering overhead. In the distance the Santa Lucia Mountains rising steeply from the sea and ranging south toward Big Sur. Jeffers was then twenty-seven years old, and a writer, though of no special promise. Una was three years his senior, a very striking woman by all accounts, small and vivid. They had been married a little over a year, and they had arrived by stagecoach. It was almost the last moment of the nineteenth century. Europe had just gone to war; the United States would be entering it within a few years.

Within a few years that astonishing explosion in American writing which came to be known as modernism would be well under way. Ezra Pound, then in London, had already published *Lustra*, Frost's *North of Boston* would appear the following year, followed by Eliot's *Prufrock and Other Observations* and Williams's *Al Que Quiere* in 1917, Moore's *Poems* in 1920, and Stevens's *Harmonium* in 1923. Jeffers's contribution to that decisive literary moment was the last to arrive. *Tamar* was published in 1924, *Roan Stallion, Tamar, and Other Poems* in 1925. The poems which gave that book its originality and force had begun to be written about five years earlier, in 1919, just after the end of the war and the Versailles peace, which issued, among the writers of Europe and America, in that curious and intense fusion of energy and despair which produced *The Wasteland* and *Soldier's Pay* and *The Sun Also Rises*.

Robinson Jeffers was thirty-two when he began to discover what he had to say and the style in which to say it. He had by then published two volumes of apprentice work, *Flagons and Apples,* 1912, and *Californians,* 1916, which even for a sympathetic and interested reader are fairly hard going: conventional in form, conventional in thought, and not especially well made. Reading them makes the leap to *Roan Stallion* seem even more surprising and unparalleled. It may have taken the poet a while to find his voice, but the voice that he found, with its long line, its suppleness and somber beauty, its sense of power and edge and prophetic risk, is unmistakable. "Natural Music" may not be the first poem in the formed style, but it is one of the earliest and it is fascinating how much of Jeffers's vision is already present in it:

> The old voice of the ocean, the bird-chatter of little rivers,
> (Winter has given them gold for silver
> To stain their water and bladed green for brown to line their
>   banks)
> From different throats intone one language.
> So I believe if we were strong enough to listen without
> Divisions of desire and terror
> To the storm of the sick nations, the rage of the hunger-
>   smitten cities,

Those voices also would be found
Clean as a child's; or like some girl's breathing who dances
    alone
By the ocean-shore, dreaming of lovers.

I remember being told in high school that if at the end of the
world, it could be wound up and played again, like a music box, it
would sound, the second time around, as innocent as the singing
of birds. I didn't wonder then if the category "innocent" applied
to birdsong or if the remark meant that the sounds of torture,
inconsolable grief, sick fear, and helpless suffering needed to be
heard as a kind of music—or, as "Natural Music" would have it,
still more intimately, as the breathing of a dancer. It almost seems
like malice, the way the last image takes the lush, romantic diction
of late nineteenth-century poetry and forces it against the most
terrible human circumstances. But that is what this poem does; it
suggests that the sound of the river and the sound of cities being
bombed—a practice that had yet to be perfected when the poem
was written—and the sound of a young girl's first vaguely sexual
longing for happiness need to be understood as a single, entirely
natural music, that the whole cycle of human desire, which is also
the cycle of human history, is in a certain way nothing, a sound on
the wind. This idea—it is ultimately a religious idea—would alter-
nately, sometimes simultaneously, torment and console Robinson
Jeffers for the rest of his life.

Mostly, at the beginning, it consoled him. Everywhere in the
work there is the sense of a man to whom the wholeness and beauty
of the world, particularly the world as seen from a rocky bluff above
Carmel Bay, and its reality, its actually being there outside his own
circle of human need, is a stunning and sobering gift:

At night, toward dawn, all the lights of the shore have died,
And the wind moves. Moves in the dark
The sleeping power of the ocean, no more beastlike than man-
    like,
Not to be compared; itself and itself.

And again:

Great-enough both accepts and subdues; the great frame takes
    all creatures;
From the greatness of their element they all take beauty.
Gulls; and the dingy freightship lurching south in the eye of
    the rain-wind;
The airplane dipping over the hill; hawks hovering,
The white grass of the headland; cormorants roosting upon the
    guano-
Whitened skerries; pelicans awind; sea-slime
Shining at night in the wave-stir . . .

All of the young moderns were deeply influenced by symbolist verse
and were also looking for a way past the cloudiness of its rhetoric,
its subjectivity and aestheticism; for Jeffers this feeling for the power
and actuality of the physical world was the way, as the poem
"Credo" makes clear:

My friend from Asia has powers and magic, he plucks a blue
    leaf from the young blue-gum
And gazing upon it, gathering and quieting
The God in his mind, creates an ocean more real than the
    ocean, the salt, the actual
Appalling presence, the power of the waters.
He believes that nothing is real except as we make it. I humbler
    have found in my blood
Bred west of the Caucasus a harder mysticism.

Multitude stands in my mind but I think that the ocean in the
    bone vault is only
The bone vault's ocean: out there is the ocean's . . .

It is not much of a jump from this assertion of the integrity and
reality of the natural world to the identification of that world with
God. It was in fact the leap that had already been taken by the
American transcendentalists. And it is one that he made soon
enough; Jeffers's is a more chilling conception than Emerson's or
Thoreau's, based as it is on the early twentieth century's picture of
the physical universe and on the status of human beings as under-
stood by evolutionary biology. The world is, and human conscious-
ness has no very special part in it, and human suffering no special
meaning. And freedom consists in understanding that. It is what he
would say in poem after poem, down to the final poem of his final
book, *The Beginning and the End:*

The wings and the wild hungers, the wave-worn skerries, the
    bright quick minnows
Living in terror to die in torment—
Man's fate and theirs—and the island rocks and immense
    ocean beyond, and Lobos
Darkening above the bay: they are beautiful?
That is their quality: not mercy, not mind, not goodness, but
    the beauty of God.

Does he begin to sound like a preacher? His father was a
Presbyterian minister and a Calvinist theologian. It seems to be the
fate of American poets to reinvent the religions of their childhoods
in their poetry. Jeffers is certainly an instance. And if he needed,
in Calvinist fashion, to believe in the perfection of God and the
absolute depravity of man, man in the twentieth century seemed to

cooperate with that need. He had before him every day the contrast between the grand theater of sundown off Point Lobos and a horror that rapidly escalated from trench warfare through the invention of aerial bombardment to Guernica, Dachau, Hiroshima, and the gulags.

Moreover, he had, like many others in his generation, read Oswald Spengler's *The Decline of the West* and other fashionable theories of culture cycles which suggested, in reaction to the cheerfully Hegelian optimism of a previous generation, that Western civilization was doomed. So it too, rising and falling, terrible as the fall was, could be seen as a phase in the rhythm of the tragic dance. This view gets stated most forcefully in "Rearmament," a poem written in about 1934, when he saw accurately that the world had begun to prepare for another war:

These grand and fatal movements toward death: the grandeur
    of the mass
Makes pity a fool, the tearing pity
For the atoms of the mass, the persons, the victims, makes it
    seem monstrous
To admire the tragic beauty they build.
It is beautiful as a river flowing or a slowly gathering
Glacier on a high mountain rock-face,
Bound to plow down a forest, or as frost in November,
The gold and flaming death-dance for leaves,
Or a girl in the night of her spent maidenhood, bleeding and
    kissing.
I would burn my right hand in a slow fire
To change the future . . . I should do foolishly. The beauty of
    modern
Man is not in the persons but in the
Disastrous rhythm, the heavy and mobile masses, the dance of
    the
Dream-led masses down the dark mountain.

None of these developments was entirely visible to the young couple looking down on Carmel in 1914. The moment has qualities both of beginning and aftermath. "When the stage-coach topped the hill," the poet recalled later, "and we looked down through pines and seafogs on Carmel, it was evident that we had come without knowing it to our inevitable place." Their arrival there had not been simple. They had met eight years before in Los Angeles. Jeffers was born in Pittsburgh, Pennsylvania, where his father was a professor of theology. He was educated partly in private schools in Pittsburgh and partly abroad—in Zurich, Lausanne, Leipzig, and Geneva, so he was fluent in German and French at the age of twelve, and he also knew Latin and Greek—and commented later on the method of instruction: "When I was nine years old, my father began to slap Latin into me, literally, with his hands." It's hard not to believe that there is some connection between this father, whom he loved deeply and unaffectedly, as far as one can tell, and the cruelly beautiful God of the later poems. But the result of his education, after the family had moved west in 1903 when Jeffers's father retired, was that he graduated from Occidental College in Los Angeles at the precocious age of eighteen.

In the fall of 1906 he began, in a desultory way, to do graduate work in comparative literature at the University of Southern California, where Una, the wife of a successful lawyer, young herself, bored by golf and hungry for poetry, had been taking courses. They met, appropriately enough, in a class on German romanticism, and they read *Faust* together. It is difficult, from the published accounts, to make out very clearly the course of their long tortuous courtship. Jeffers left that winter for the University of Zurich but returned the following fall to try medical studies at USC. Una meanwhile continued to work on her B.A. and then on a master's degree. She wrote a thesis entitled, "The Enduring Element of Mysticism in

Man." In *Robinson Jeffers: Poet of California*, James Karman quotes one particularly interesting passage. "In certain centuries," she wrote, "the souls of men seem to be stirring and wakening after long sleep, and tentatively trying in a thousand different ways to break through the crust of the material which encompasses them: at such times we see men restless, troubled, striving for they scarcely know what."

This probably catches something of Una Kuster's state of mind in those years and something of the febrile spirit at the beginning of the new century; it must also reflect the state of mind of her intense and drifting poet lover. It certainly demonstrates the way the pair influenced each other. A sudden, Nietzschean pronouncement which leaps out of the early narrative "Roan Stallion" seems to borrow from Una's prose directly:

> Humanity is the start of
>   the race; I say
> Humanity is the mold to break away from, the crust to break
>   through, the coal to break into fire,
> The atom to be split.
>   Tragedy that breaks man's face and a white
>   fire flies out; vision that fools him
> Out of his limits, desire that fools him out of his limits, unnatu-
>   ral crime, inhuman science,
> Slit eyes in the mask . . .

In the fall of 1910, apparently in an effort to break off the affair, Jeffers left Los Angeles and enrolled in forestry studies at the University of Washington in Seattle. Part of his motive may have been attraction to "inhuman science," but he seems mostly to have been floundering toward a profession. Wallace Stevens was at about this time trying to talk his father into letting him try the impractical career of a journalist. William Carlos Williams was about to start a medical practice. T. S. Eliot would soon and rather reluctantly try to please his parents by embarking on graduate work in philosophy. Only Ezra Pound flaunted silk scarves and lived by his wits. Jeffers was then twenty-three; interestingly, his mother and father accompanied him to Seattle, "to make a home," his mother said, "for Robin." By 1911 he was back in California, drinking a lot and at a loss.

Una had gone to Europe at her husband's suggestion to think things over. She was courted there by a man—he sounds as if he were invented by Henry James—called Percy Peacock. What a small world it must have been. The biographies actually quote an interview from the *Los Angeles Times* in which Una's husband Teddy Kuster gives his view of the affair: "She turned to philosophy and the school of modern decadents," he explained to a reporter, "and she talked of things beyond the ken of those who dwelt upon the lower levels." In the spring of 1912 Jeffers had a volume of his verse, *Flagons and Apples,* privately published. It is very much in the style of modern decadents like Arthur Symons and Ernest Dowson, sensual and world-weary and, in truth, fairly awful; even its young author seems to have thought so.

And then—as in the silent movies, which were beginning to be made in nearby Hollywood—everything unraveled toward a happy ending. Una returned from Europe to find that Teddy had fallen in love (with an eighteen-year-old, Una's age when she met him) and was now willing to file for divorce. Robin had just had a short story—very urbane in manner—accepted by a fashionable magazine, *The Smart Set.* More crucially, he had come into "a modest legacy" of $10,000 on the death of a distant relative. They were married on August 2, 1913.

Ten months later—the Furies did not visit on them the large-scale catastrophes suffered by the characters in Jeffers's poems, but they inflicted a quieter and more common cruelty—they lost their first child, a girl named Maeve, who was born and died on May 5, 1914. And at the end of that year, in December, while Robin and Una were exploring the Big Sur coast for the first time, they received news of the death of Dr. Jeffers.

But whatever grief they nursed through that summer or the following winter, they had come to Carmel-by-the-Sea, as it was then called, to start a new life, and they began it with great energy. That the life came to have the quality of myth was not an accident. They were a romantic young couple, and they had acted a great drama together. They wanted to live in an original way, and like many young artists they set about it consciously. Later, at the height of the fame of Robinson Jeffers (and he became very famous: his face appeared on the cover of *Time* in the early thirties and *Vogue* did a story on the family; he was exactly the magazines' idea of a poet, unlike the studious Eliot or the cranky unintelligible Pound), their story was one that many people came to know: how these adulterous lovers had broken with convention and gone to a remote spot on the California coast and built themselves a stone cottage by the sea to which they gave the name of Tor House; how Robin, having learned the art of masonry, built Una a tower, called Hawk Tower, beside the house, the tower inspired by his wife's love of the Irish poet Yeats, the stones hauled by hand from the Pacific shore; that they had twin sons, Garth and Donnan; that they lived a life a little apart, idyllic, solitary, pastoral; and that there, in the house by the Pacific, the poet broke through the conventions of nineteenth-century poetry and wrote great, long-lined, turbulent poems, full of the rhythms of the sea and as cold and passionate and morally indifferent as the sea itself.

There are several things wrong with this picture, though there is some truth in it. Carmel was, for one thing, a less remote place than it might have seemed. It already had some reputation as an artist's colony. In fact, the year before the Jefferses arrived, Jack London had published a novel, serialized in *Cosmopolitan*, called *Valley of the Moon*, which describes and affectionately satirizes life in Carmel and the group of artists who settled there. They were mostly California writers: George Sterling, a San Francisco poet; Mary Austen, who later wrote a small classic about the southern deserts, *Land of Little Rain*; Upton Sinclair. Other writers came and went: Sinclair Lewis, Lincoln Steffens. Jack London's version of the town is interesting partly because it catches the attitudes of the art crowd circa 1912. His tactic is to let a pair of working-class lovers, she a laundress, he a teamster and ex-prizefighter, wander into town looking for a better life than the one of bitter toil they have known. Among the golden-tongued and privileged inhabitants of Carmel, who seem to be living in a beautiful place and in exquisite freedom, Saxon, the heroine of the novel, is puzzled:

> But what she could not comprehend was the pessimism that so often cropped up. The wild Irish playwright had terrible spells of depression. The poet Shelley, who also wrote vaudeville turns in his concrete cell, was a chronic pessimist. St. John, a young magazine writer, was an anarchist disciple of Nietzsche. Masson, a painter, held to a doctrine of eternal recurrence that was petrifying. And Hall, usually so merry, could outfoot them all when he got started on the cosmic pathos of religion and the gibbering anthropomorphisms of those who loved not to die. Saxon was oppressed by these sad children of art. It was inconceivable that they, of all people, should be so forlorn.

It seems a summary of Jeffers's themes, composed seven or eight years before he came to them.

Una's letters provide another look at Carmel a few years later. James Karman quotes one which suggests a rather lively and toney social scene:

> We went to an amusing dinner party there at Bechdolt's the other night. The Jimmy Hoppers were there and the Lloyd Osbornes. He, you know, is Stevenson's step-son. They live part of the year at an interesting country place near Gilroy—the other part in New York, London, and Paris. They were in France and London last winter—Jimmy Hopper has been two years at the front and left here last week on his way to France again for *Colliers.* Lots of war talk. No end of interesting people here—The other night when we were dressing for dinner Robin said "What to wear?" and I said his good-looking riding suit—and I'd wear a dinner gown. People dress so queerly here—one of us would be fixed right—sure enough. Osborne big and gray and massively English was in golf clothes—she, his young second wife in a black chiffon velvet very low with Paris written all over it.
>
> Some weeks ago we went to (a big) dinner at the Hoppers served in the garden—the Hoppers have George Sterling's house. The piece de resistance was *mussels* which the Wilson chef prepared right before our eyes over an outdoor fireplace. The Wilsons are the *Harry Leon Wilsons*—you know his magazine stories. They have a big place down the coast—a chef, gardeners, chauffeurs, outdoor swimming pool and that kind of thing. Mrs. W. is stunning—to look at—stunning *interesting* clothes.—His first wife is Rose O'Neil—(the Kewpie creator, you know—). Everyone here has ex-es so I am quite unnoticed about that—anyway no one knows it I guess.

Jeffers can't have liked the social round very much. He had had a rather solitary childhood and was, as an adult, taciturn and—

many observers reported—painfully shy. But Carmel was not a wild and desolate refuge, however solitary the poet chose to be. He and Una did have twin sons in 1916; she went south to Pasadena to be near a family physician for the delivery. And in 1918 they bought the Tor House property and began to build the cottage. The site was then two miles from the village; work began in the summer of 1919. Jeffers worked with the mason, writing in the morning—this was the period of his breakthrough to the *Tamar* poems—and doing physical labor in the afternoons; and he planted some two thousand trees on the property, eucalyptus and cypress and pine. Most of these are gone now, but the house, set among other, more modern and more expensive coastal houses, still stands; it is beautifully modest, with windows facing the sea, low ceilings with heavy, polished beams, and an exquisite cottage garden of heather and beach wildflowers, and herbs. The tower, which was built between 1920 and 1924, is a witty, small building, constructed in a spirit of play, with a lookout in the top, and a dungeon, and a secret passageway for the boys to play in.

There are poems which suggest a rich domestic life—"household verses," the poet called them. And, forty years past their arrival in Carmel, when he was almost seventy and Una dead of cancer, it was this vision of their life that the old poet both fiercely and sentimentally recalled:

> Una is still alive.
> A few years back we are making love greedy as hawks,
> A boy and a married girl. A few years back
> We are still young, strong-shouldered, joyfully laboring
> To make our house. Then she, in the wide sea-window,
> Endlessly enduring but not very patient,
> Teaches our sons to read. She is still there,

Her beautiful pale face, heavy hair, great eyes
Bent to the book.

Many poems—like "The Deer Lay Down Their Bones," which is among his best—testify to the depth of his love for his wife and the life they shared. But this should not obscure the fact that in 1915 Jeffers was in many ways a confused and deeply pained and unhappy man, or the fact that he wrote in the end a poetry that feels deeply lonely and tormented.

The reasons for his confusion were clear enough. He felt he had gotten nowhere in his art. *Californians,* published in 1916, was not very well received and, though it is an advance over *Flagons and Apples,* he himself recognized that it was derivative, that he hadn't found his way yet. He writes about this time with charming candor in a 1935 preface to the Modern Library reissue of *Roan Stallion.* He is walking in the woods and falls into "bitter meditation":

> It had occurred to me that I was already a year older than Keats when he died, and I too had written many verses, but they were all worthless. I had imitated and imitated, and that was all . . .
>
> When I set down the dog and went back over our bridge for the bundle of firewood my thoughts began to be more practical, not more pleasant. This originality, without which a writer of verses is only a verse-writer, is there any way to attain it? The more advanced contemporary poets were attaining it by going farther and farther along the way that perhaps Mallarmé's aging dream had shown them, divorcing poetry from reason and ideas, bringing it nearer to music, finally to astonish the world with what would look like pure nonsense and would be pure poetry. No doubt these lucky writers were imitating each other instead of imitating Shelley and Milton as I had done . . . but no, not all of them, someone must be setting the pace, going farther than anyone had dared to go before. Ezra Pound perhaps? Whoever it was, was *original* . . .

But now, as I smelled the wild honey midway the trestle and meditated the direction of modern poetry, my discouragement blackened. It seemed to me that Mallarmé and his followers, renouncing intelligibility in order to concentrate the music of poetry, had turned off the road into a narrowing lane. Their successors could only make further renunciations; ideas had gone, now meter had gone, imagery would have to go; then recognizable emotions would have to go; perhaps at last words might have to go or give up their meaning, nothing be left but musical syllables. Every advance required the elimination of some aspect of reality, and what could it profit me to know the direction of modern literature if I did not like the direction? It was too much like putting out one's eyes to cultivate the sense of hearing, or cutting off the right hand to develop the left. These austerities were not for me . . .

I laid down the bundle of sticks and stood sadly by the bridgehead. The sea-fog was coming up the ravine, fingering through the pines, the air smelled of the sea and pine-resin and yerba buena, my girl and my dog were with me . . . and I was standing there like a God-forsaken man-of-letters, making my final decision not to become a "modern." I did not want to become slight and fantastic, abstract and unintelligible.

I was doomed to go on imitating dead men, unless some impossible wind should blow me emotions or ideas, or a point of view, or even mere rhythms, that had not occurred to them. There was nothing to do about it . . .

That impossible wind came to Robinson Jeffers three or four years after the moment he describes. The romantic Una spoke of it as "an awakening such as adolescents and religious converts experience" and attributed it partly to a strength her husband absorbed from handling stone. In fact, it is not clear what happened. There is as much evidence to argue for a gradual evolution as there is for a sudden revelation. At least at the level of style, it is possible to watch the long, characteristic, free verse line emerge from the metrical experimentation in the early lyrics and narratives.

It derives, I think, not from Whitman, as so many critics have assumed, but from the long-lined dactylic and anapestic experiments of the late Victorian poets like Swinburne. Jeffers wrote some song-like lyrics in about 1917 that illustrate the point. One of them begins:

> Was it lovely to lie among violets ablossom in the valleys of love
> on the breast of the south?
> It was lovely but lovelier now
> To behold the calm head of the dancer we dreaded, his curls
> are as tendrils of the vineyard, O Death.

The lilt of it is almost ludicrously exaggerated: was it *lov*ely to *lie* among *vio*lets a*blossom* in the *val*leys of *love* on the *breast* of the *south?* But it is not hard to see how the long line of a poem like "Continent's End" derives from it:

> At the equinox when the earth was veiled in a late rain,
> wreathed with wet poppies, waiting spring,
> The ocean swelled for a far storm and beat its boundary, the
> ground-swell shook the beds of granite.

It is much more a sobering up of Victorian verse, a suppression of those rocking-horse rhythms that the prepositional phrase invites into the English language, than it is a leap to Whitman's exhilarated and playful long line. And for a writer who loved the prose of Thomas Hardy—there is a stone in Tor House on which the poet paused in his labors to carve the fact of Hardy's death on a day in 1924—that sober and rhythmic line had the virtue of being very well suited to realistic narrative, like the beginning of "Roan Stallion":

> The dog barked; then the woman stood in the doorway, and
> > hearing iron strike stone down the steep road
> Covered her head with a black shawl and entered the light
> > rain; she stood at the turn of the road.

You can hear, particularly in this last line, a varying and doubling of the light, anapestic rhythm: *cov*ered her *head* with a *black shawl* and *ent*ered the *light rain:* she *stood* at the *turn* of the *road.*

And beyond these technical considerations, it is possible to watch the evolution of the poet's sense of how to speak from where he was in the world, the development of what came to be the myth of himself: the man who at the end of a culture cycle stood at continent's end beside a house and tower he had built himself and told his culture bitter truths.

This aspect of his transformation in the early 1920s does suggest not slow change but a bolt of lightning, a *gnosis.* If he did not have a vision, he had a series of insights that came to have the quality of a vision. There is first of all a sense of terrible and tormenting violence at the center of life, from the hawk's claw to the fury of war to the slow decay of stone. And there was also a sense, sharply, of something pained, divided and deeply sick in the human heart, at the root of sexual desire and religious longing. And finally there was the leap—to the wholeness of things, a leap out of the human and its pained and diseased desiring into the permanence and superb indifference of nature. The possibility of this leap became at first the central wish and, finally, the doctrine of his poetry.

Speculating about the origin of it has occupied his biographers and critics. His father was an older man when he married his mother, and some have guessed that they created for the poet an Oedipal conflict which he acted out by stealing Una from her husband, and that the guilt of that transgression fuels the poems. Others have argued that it was divisions of desire that he experienced after the marriage—William Everson has speculated that he had other relationships in the period between 1917 and 1919—that led both to the yearning identification with stone and the torment of guilt. And it has been pointed out that in the poems the very violence of the western landscape, geologically young, haunted by a sense of recent and prehuman catastrophe, seems to tease his mind toward such an insight. Still others have observed its connection with Calvinism, with the philosophy of Schopenhauer and the German romantics that he absorbed as a boy at school. In any case, it is an ancient movement of the soul—from anguish at life to the idea of God.

When the poet himself attempted to speak about what happened to him, he did so in a poetry reading at Harvard University in 1941—it will tell you how much the world has changed to know that it was his *first* poetry reading; he was fifty-four years old—and he singled out the vision of Orestes in his verse drama, *The Tower Beyond Tragedy*. As in Aeschylus, Orestes has, at his sister's urging, killed his mother to avenge his father's death. In Jeffers's version of the story, once the pair have isolated themselves by their crime, when they are in some sense beyond crime, Electra offers herself to her brother. It is Nietzschean, I suppose: beyond good and evil; it is also a metaphor for the mirroring and inward-turning of human desire, mixed up with crime against the parents. There is evidence that Jeffers had been reading Freud, but the passage doesn't feel like the application of an idea got out of a book; it dramatizes the poet's own sense, shared with Freud, that human desire is fundamentally incestuous and blind. Orestes refuses his sister. What is most haunting about the way that he does so is, for me, the glimpse it contains of Jeffers's own moment of vision. Electra, spurned, threatens suicide. Orestes is unmoved. "I have," he says, "fallen in love outward."

The verse Orestes speaks, he told the Harvard audience, was intended to express "the feeling—I will say the certitude—that the world, the universe, is one being, a single organism, one great life that includes all life and all things, and is so beautiful it must be loved and reverenced, and in moments of mystical vision we identify ourselves with it." By then his doctrine of inhumanism, as he called it, was well known and associated with his isolationist's opposition to the war in Europe. He knew his audience did not like much of what he stood for. His verses, he said, "also express a protest against human narcissism." He elaborated: "The whole human race spends too much emotion on itself. The happiest and freest man is the scientist investigating nature, or the artist admiring it, the person who is interested in things that are not human. Or if he is interested in human things, let him regard them objectively, as a small part of a great music. Certainly humanity has claims, on all of us; we can best fulfill them by keeping our emotional sanity and this by seeing around and beyond the human race."

These are the cooler reflections of the older man. What happened to the Jeffers of the nineteen-twenties was that he began to write like a demon, like a man possessed. First came "Tamar," a narrative of some sixty pages, then "The Tower Beyond Tragedy," fifty pages, and "Roan Stallion," fifteen pages, followed by "The Women at Point Sur," which is the length of a novel, and the hundred pages of "Cawdor," plus sixty or so lyric poems. This by 1928. Readers of this volume can get a sense of the explosion of work by reading in succession "Orestes to Electra," "Roan Stallion," "Prelude," "The Old Man's Dream After He Died," and "The Caged Eagle's Death Dream." Jeffers kept up this pace without interruption from about 1920 to 1938, when his *Selected Poems* was published. He wrote in the course of those eighteen years fifteen narrative poems ranging in length from ten to two hundred pages, four verse dramas, and almost two hundred lyric poems.

The narratives, like the world they were written in, seemed to become more strained and violent each year, but the life they came out of was uneventful enough. Jeffers's sudden fame intensified his shyness. He wrote. Una ran the household. She was apparently a vigorously maternal figure. Some time during this period her former husband Teddy Kuster showed up in Carmel and had built, not far from the Jefferses, his own larger and more expensive version of their stone cottage. Una befriended his wife—Edith Greenan, who later wrote a biography of her friend, *Of Una Jeffers*—and was in and out of both houses. She raised her boys and saw to it, according to observers, that Robin kept busy. In her gossipy memoir, *Una and Robin*, Mabel Dodge Luhan gives this rather amusing glimpse of breakfast at the Jefferses':

> "Now, dear, you'd better go upstairs," Una says. Robin is always held a little below the surface in the morning, and Una leaves him to it. He isn't taciturn—he is dazed to the outer world. His pulse beats slowly, and his eyes seem to see inwards. He is aware of his three, and would be responsive if they wanted him. He would always give up poetry for life—his life. He would rather drive the boys to school than write a poem—thinking life more valuable than its reflection; but Una won't have it. "Now go upstairs, Robin," Una says, briskly.

Jeffers paced as he worked in the bedroom above the kitchen; other observers report that when Una did not hear the characteristic sound of his shuffle, she would rap on the ceiling with a broom.

During those years they took one trip abroad, visiting the British Isles from June to December of 1929. *Descent to the Dead*, which contains some of Jeffers's best work and is interesting for its resemblance to the work of some younger poets—to Seamus Heaney's *North*, in particular, and to some of the work of Ted Hughes—dates from that long vacation; and they spent some part of most summers with Mabel Dodge Luhan in Taos, New Mexico. But mostly they were at home in the quiet of their Carmel life where Jeffers, as the world lurched toward war, poured out poems that were increasingly nightmarish and misanthropic. This passage from the short narrative, "Margrave," published in 1932, shows the extremity of the vision. The poem pauses in its telling and urges the stars to flee the infection of human consciousness, then looks forward to the day when the sun rises over the dust to which time and the weather have reduced the last human skulls:

> Then the sun will say "What ailed me a moment?" and resume
> The old soulless triumph, and the iron and stone earth
> With confident and inorganic glory obliterate
> Her ruins and fossils, like that incredible unfading rose
> Of desert in Arizona glowing life to scorn,
> And grind the chalky emptied seed-shells of consciousness
> The bare skulls of the dead to powder; after some million
> Courses around the sun her sadness may pass

And against this fury—which always feels a good deal like self-loathing—there is always the life outside of his life, through which, as in the best of these poems, like "The Purse-Seine," the poet tried to reconcile himself to the coming catastrophe and to his own death.

By 1938 the twenty-year torrent of verse seemed to have come to an end and Jeffers was emotionally exhausted. The strain told, as it often does, in his marriage. That summer at Mabel Dodge Luhan's he seems to have had an affair, and when Una heard of it she tried to kill herself. In his account of the incident, James Karman suggests a shaky but nevertheless real recovery. Una had always been passionately possessive. Jeffers always seems to have admired—and been slightly appalled by—the fierceness of her spirit. Meanwhile, the *Selected Poems* appeared and it became evident that the poet had left much of his audience behind. The vision was too dark, the narratives on which his reputation seemed to rest were often repellently violent and hysterical, and the politics were deeply out of fashion, at least among people who were likely to read poems. Jeffers seems to have been, politically and sentimentally, an old-fashioned Jeffersonian republican. He believed in the American republic as a commonwealth of independent and self-reliant households, and saw himself—educated at a time when small boys knew the history of Rome and had been taught the parallels between the Roman and American republics—as a defender of the spartan and honest American commonweal against the thickening of the empire. He seems to have wanted his country to be, as he wanted his poems to be, as cool and aloof as a hawk from what was going forward, the inevitable and horrifying collapse of European civilization.

Though this may have been philosophical conviction, it did not in practice appear to differ very much from the view of any wealthy, Republican, Roosevelt-hating citizen of Carmel, living on private income and insulated from the effects of the Depression, and so it did not endear him to the predominantly liberal, socialist, and humanist literary culture of the thirties and forties. The work of the war years is intensely dispirited. This must be due partly to the trouble in his marriage, but the poems are also the work of a man sickened by the war, by political processes so-called and by the human race. American patriotism sickened him as much as German or Japanese patriotism, and it brought him soon enough into conflict not just with popular opinion, but with his publisher.

When the editors at Random House saw *The Double Axe* in 1948, they balked. After persuading Jeffers to omit ten of the most offensive and blatantly editorial poems—which treated Churchill and Roosevelt as morally equivalent to Hitler and Mussolini—they published the book with an editorial disclaimer on the back cover and a preface by Jeffers somewhat wearily explaining the philosophy of inhumanism. There is something to be said for the bitterness and bluntness of the poems of this period—I have included one of the group that he omitted from *The Double Axe*, "War-Guilt Trials," mainly for its peremptory glance aside at the scandal surrounding Ezra Pound—but Jeffers himself seemed to be, at the very least, discouraged by the task they undertook. As he said in the preface to *Be Angry at the Sun* in 1941:

> . . . I wish to lament the obsession with contemporary history that pins many of these pieces to the calendar, like butterflies to cardboard. Poetry is not private monologue, but I think it is not public speech either; and in general it is the worse for being timely . . .
>
> Yet it is right that a man's views be expressed, though the poetry suffer for it. Poetry should represent the whole mind; if part of the mind is occupied unhappily, so much the worse. And no use postponing the poetry to a time when the storms may have passed, for I think we have but seen a beginning of them; the calm to look for is the calm at the whirlwind's heart.

The postwar years brought the Jeffers family other things to think about. Before the furor over *The Double Axe*, there had been the immense public success of Jeffers's adaptation of Euripides's *Medea*, which he had undertaken for his friend Judith Anderson and which opened on Broadway in 1947. And in 1949 the cancer for which Una had been treated from 1941 to 1944 returned; it had spread to her spine. She lingered for some time, nursed by her husband and her son Donnan and daughter-in-law Lee in her room at Tor House. She died on September 1, 1950, in her husband's presence. *Hungerfield* is the book of his grief, with its peculiar title poem, the tender and moving elegy for his wife framing the brutal narrative. The book was published in 1954. Jeffers was then sixty-seven, and his sadness seems to have quickened his imagination, or altered its focus, as he began the work of his last years. The poems in *The Beginning and the End* belong to the increasingly rich American poetry of old age, and it is various enough to make one wish that the poet had been less obsessed and single-minded in his earlier years. The mind has relaxed somewhat. Though he still hammers away at his religious convictions, he is able to accommodate more wayward observations than he had permitted himself in the furious poetry of the 1930s and 1940s.

He died in January of 1962. Some of the land around the house had been sold off to pay taxes. The house itself had by then been electrified and acquired a telephone. Most of the trees he planted had been cut down, replaced by suburban houses with large bay windows gawking toward the sea like the open mouths of baby birds. At the end his disgust with the encroachment was moderate. He seems to have felt that he had had, on the whole, a good life. His poetry at his death was far from forgotten, but he no longer occupied the commanding place in American letters he had seemed permanently to have carved out thirty years before. And it is hard to believe that it was in the end a matter of much consequence to him. He had had his say.

His centenary seems an appropriate time to reconsider his achievement. The least that can be said of it is that he wrote many remarkable and original poems. He was not afraid to stake a large claim. Critics have been inclined to expound his ideas systematically, but it seems to me that he is, in the end, an intuitive, unsystematic, and contradictory thinker. It is as a feeler not a thinker that he matters. Looking out at the Pacific landscape, with its sense of primitive violence that time and the weather had not quietened and eroded, he found himself haunted by the riddles of desire and suffering, and he thought he saw a way out of the cycle, and that way connected to his almost mute, though intense, feeling for the natural world—for all the life outside of and imperiled by the rapacity and unconsciousness of the human usurpation of the planet. He came to feel, with tragic clarity, that human beings could be saved, if they could be saved, only by what they were destroying. This is his moral side, the Cassandra voice. As a poet he kept trying to make images from the movements, serene and terrible, of the life around him for what he had discovered or intuited—for the power at the center of life which reconciled him to its cruelty. One feels him straining toward it, toward what is not human in the cold salt of the Pacific and the great sundowns and the rocks and the hawk's curved, efficient beak. It is in the farthest reaches of this intuitive straining that one feels most in Jeffers the presence of a great poet. And this is the dimension of his work that the poet Alan Williamson had in mind when he identified the poetic tradition to which Jeffers belongs: "Jeffers belongs, with Rilke, with Mallarmé, with Whitman and Hart Crane, to the project of inventing a spirituality which can survive the death of Christianity; inventing, as Jung and Heinrich Zimmer have said, an equivalent of Buddhism which is not Buddhism, but something distinctively Western."

Jeffers's refusal to become a modernist gives him another interest, which is his willingness to speak his mind. It is this aspect of his work that most bothered critics in mid-century. They were busy absorbing the modernist aesthetic: Go in fear of general ideas, Pound had said, the natural object is always an adequate symbol of the idea or the inward state. There is much to be said for this view: It is a way of bringing the minimum of conceptual baggage to the fresh encounter with reality. What was death to Stevens? A flock of pigeons which made ambiguous undulations as they went downward to darkness on extended wings. What was the secret principle of order in things to Ezra Pound? A rose in the steel dust. What was the paradise, tucked in memory or hidden just beyond misery, to T. S. Eliot? Sunlight and laughter in a garden. Partly these images have immense and memorable evocative power. Partly they have the permanent sphinx-like and hermetic quality of all metaphor. And one feels in them man in the twentieth century pounding on the wall of what he cannot know. This was the context in which Jeffers, risking the banality and lameness of the general statement— and achieving them often enough—said it out, tried to speak what he knew in the language of his time.

There is much to be said against his work, and most of it has been said. The younger generation of California poets, Yvor Winters in the thirties and Kenneth Rexroth in the forties, anxious to dispose of the overwhelming figure down the coast, wrote scathing and not inaccurate criticism of his work. Jeffers can be pretentious, repetitious, bombastic, humorless, fuzzy. The most dangerous thing that can be said of him, I think, is that he was verbally careless. Language itself is simply not one of Jeffers's subjects. He can write "the weed-clad rocks," which no other poet of his generation would do—because they would not wish the rocks to appear "dressed" and because the figure is, anyway, a cliché. Jeffers uses the phrase because it came to hand. He can write, in the same poem, about "the black lips of the height" and "the thin sleeve of the sea" and not be troubled by the scrambled images he inadvertently calls up.

All of which is to say that he is imperfect, but the other truth is that he is more interesting than many more careful writers, partly because he was driven by strange expedients: who else would have tried to describe the last moment of an already dead eagle's living instincts, or the last flickering consciousness in the separate cells of a decomposing brain? Or attempted a poem as peculiar and distraught as "Prelude," with its crucified hawk and its landscape of tormented sexual longing? In the first narrative in this book the Indian woman California yearns toward a horse, which is an emblem of the beast- and god-like power and beauty of life itself, and at the end of the poem, out of an obscure human loyalty to a husband she does not even like—a loyalty that Jeffers the philosopher would have disavowed and one that the poem makes necessary and right—she kills the animal. In the last narrative, the brutal man Hungerfield, furious with the black angel of death which has dared to invade his house and take the mother who despised him, wrestles death to a standstill. And this story, repellent, psychologically false somehow as the narratives can often be, written in the spirit of a tender gift to his dead and beloved wife, haunts the reader. Everywhere, and usually when one feels least comfortable, one feels the presence of a truly obsessed and original imagination.

The experiments in narrative, mythic and realistic, continue to be relevant. I've tried to include as many of the shorter ones as possible, but I think, finally, that Jeffers is strongest in the descriptive and meditative lyrics. There his directness gave him the old power of poetry—not to say what no one else had ever thought, but to say what everyone has thought and felt. It is surprising in a writer who wished to be so contrary, but reading him again, reading "The Purse-Seine," for example, I was struck by how much it seemed to say what anyone has thought who has ever stood on a height and contemplated a modern city. We have lived in a catastrophic time. The redundancy of violence and suffering, the sheer immensity of the danger, always threatens to wither the imagination, to make us turn back to the purely personal, as if it were somehow more real because the mind can, at least, compass it, whereas the effort to think about the fate of the planet, about what man is that he has done to himself all the terrible things that he has done in this century, comes to us mostly as dark and private musings. And it is just this that Jeffers sought in the verse of his short poems, an art to speak those musings largely, to claim for the clear mind that needs to compass the madness the central voice of poetry.

A Note on the Text

The texts in this book for poems published up to 1938 are based on the 1938 *Selected Poems,* if they appeared in that volume. Other early poems use the text of their first printing in book form, with one exception: "Prelude" is taken from the 1968 Liveright edition of *The Women at Point Sur,* edited from the original manuscript by Tim Hunt. (This because the original poem contained a few lines which the editors at Boni & Liveright felt to be too racy in 1928 and which Jeffers reluctantly changed.) For poems published after 1938, the text of the first book appearance has been used. "War-Guilt Trials," one of the so-called suppressed poems of 1948, is the text from the 1977 Liveright edition of *The Double Axe,* edited by Bill Hotchkiss. Two scholars of Jeffers, James Karman and Tim Hunt, were extremely generous in sharing with me their work on the poet. Mr. Hunt is in the process of editing a critical edition of

Jeffers's collected works for Stanford University Press, and I could not have proceeded without his generous help. Thanks also to Lee Jeffers for a morning's hospitality in the sunlit kitchen of Tor House on a fall day, and to George L. White of the Tor House Foundation for encouragement and suggestions. I'm also grateful to Robert Pinsky and Brenda Hillman for their reading of the manuscript.

FROM

TAMAR

# NATURAL MUSIC

The old voice of the ocean, the bird-chatter of little rivers,
(Winter has given them gold for silver
To stain their water and bladed green for brown to line their
    banks)
From different throats intone one language.
So I believe if we were strong enough to listen without
Divisions of desire and terror
To the storm of the sick nations, the rage of the hunger-smitten
    cities,
Those voices also would be found
Clean as a child's; or like some girl's breathing who dances
    alone
By the ocean-shore, dreaming of lovers.

Point Joe has teeth and has torn ships; it has fierce and solitary
    beauty;
Walk there all day you shall see nothing that will not make part
    of a poem.

I saw the spars and planks of shipwreck on the rocks, and
    beyond the desolate
Sea-meadows rose the warped wind-bitten van of the pines, a
    fog-bank vaulted

Forest and all, the flat sea-meadows at that time of year were
    plated
Golden with the low flower called footsteps of the spring,
    millions of flowerets,

Whose light suffused upward into the fog flooded its vault, we
    wandered
Through a weird country where the light beat up from
    earthward, and was golden.

One other moved there, an old Chinaman gathering seaweed
    from the sea-rocks,
He brought it in his basket and spread it flat to dry on the edge
    of the meadow.

Permanent things are what is needful in a poem, things temporally
Of great dimension, things continually renewed or always
    present.

Grass that is made each year equals the mountains in her past
    and future;
Fashionable and momentary things we need not see nor speak
    of.

Man gleaning food between the solemn presences of land and
    ocean,
On shores where better men have shipwrecked, under fog and
    among flowers,

Equals the mountains in his past and future; that glow from the
    earth was only
A trick of nature's, one must forgive nature a thousand graceful
    subtleties.

THE CYCLE

The clapping blackness of the wings of pointed cormorants, the
    great indolent planes
Of autumn pelicans nine or a dozen strung shorelong,
But chiefly the gulls, the cloud-calligraphers of windy spirals
    before a storm,
Cruise north and south over the sea-rocks and over
That bluish enormous opal; very lately these alone, these and
    the clouds
And westering lights of heaven, crossed it; but then
A hull with standing canvas crept about Point Lobos . . . now
    all day long the steamers
Smudge the opal's rim; often a seaplane troubles
The sea-wind with its throbbing heart. These will increase, the
    others diminish; and later
These will diminish; our Pacific has pastured
The Mediterranean torch and passed it west across the
    fountains of the morning;
And the following desolation that feeds on Crete
Feed here; the clapping blackness of the wings of pointed
    cormorants, the great sails
Of autumn pelicans, the gray sea-going gulls,
Alone will streak the enormous opal, the earth have peace like
    the broad water, our blood's
Unrest have doubled to Asia and be peopling
Europe again, or dropping colonies at the morning star: what
    moody traveler
Wanders back here, watches the sea-fowl circle

The old sea-granite and cemented granite with one regard, and
    greets my ghost,
One temper with the granite, bulking about here?

TO THE STONE-CUTTERS

Stone-cutters fighting time with marble, you foredefeated
Challengers of oblivion
Eat cynical earnings, knowing rock splits, records fall down,
The square-limbed Roman letters
Scale in the thaws, wear in the rain. The poet as well
Builds his monument mockingly;
For man will be blotted out, the blithe earth die, the brave sun
Die blind and blacken to the heart:
Yet stones have stood for a thousand years, and pained
    thoughts found
The honey of peace in old poems.

SALMON-FISHING

The days shorten, the south blows wide for showers now,
The south wind shouts to the rivers,
The rivers open their mouths and the salt salmon
Race up into the freshet.
In Christmas month against the smoulder and menace
Of a long angry sundown,
Red ash of the dark solstice, you see the anglers,
Pitiful, cruel, primeval,
Like the priests of the people that built Stonehenge,
Dark silent forms, performing
Remote solemnities in the red shallows
Of the river's mouth at the year's turn,
Drawing landward their live bullion, the bloody mouths
And scales full of the sunset
Twitch on the rocks, no more to wander at will
The wild Pacific pasture nor wanton and spawning
Race up into fresh water.

TO THE HOUSE

I am heaping the bones of the old mother
To build us a hold against the host of the air;
Granite the blood-heat of her youth
Held molten in hot darkness against the heart
Hardened to temper under the feet
Of the ocean cavalry that are maned with snow
And march from the remotest west.
This is the primitive rock, here in the wet
Quarry under the shadow of waves
Whose hollows mouthed the dawn; little house each stone
Baptized from that abysmal font
The sea and the secret earth gave bonds to affirm you.

TO THE ROCK THAT WILL BE A CORNERSTONE OF THE HOUSE

Old garden of grayish and ochre lichen,
How long a time since the brown people who have vanished
    from here
Built fires beside you and nestled by you
Out of the ranging sea-wind? A hundred years, two hundred,
You have been dissevered from humanity
And only known the stubble squirrels and the headland rabbits,
Or the long-fetlocked plowhorses
Breaking the hilltop in December, sea-gulls following,
Screaming in the black furrow; no one
Touched you with love, the gray hawk and the red hawk
    touched you
Where now my hand lies. So I have brought you
Wine and white milk and honey for the hundred years of
    famine
And the hundred cold ages of sea-wind.

I did not dream the taste of wine could bind with granite,
Nor honey and milk please you; but sweetly
They mingle down the storm-worn cracks among the mosses,
Interpenetrating the silent
Wing-prints of ancient weathers long at peace, and the older
Scars of primal fire, and the stone
Endurance that is waiting millions of years to carry
A corner of the house, this also destined.

Lend me the stone strength of the past and I will lend you
The wings of the future, for I have them.
How dear you will be to me when I too grow old, old comrade.

Wise men in their bad hours have envied
The little people making merry like grasshoppers
In spots of sunlight, hardly thinking
Backward but never forward, and if they somehow
Take hold upon the future they do it
Half asleep, with the tools of generation
Foolishly reduplicating
Folly in thirty-year periods; they eat and laugh too,
Groan against labors, wars and partings,
Dance, talk, dress and undress; wise men have pretended
The summer insects enviable;
One must indulge the wise in moments of mockery.
Strength and desire possess the future,
The breed of the grasshopper shrills, "What does the future
Matter, we shall be dead?" Ah, grasshoppers,
Death's a fierce meadowlark: but to die having made
Something more equal to the centuries
Than muscle and bone, is mostly to shed weakness.
The mountains are dead stone, the people
Admire or hate their stature, their insolent quietness,
The mountains are not softened nor troubled
And a few dead men's thoughts have the same temper.

While this America settles in the mould of its vulgarity, heavily
    thickening to empire,
And protest, only a bubble in the molten mass, pops and sighs
    out, and the mass hardens,

I sadly smiling remember that the flower fades to make fruit, the
    fruit rots to make earth.
Out of the mother; and through the spring exultances, ripeness
    and decadence; and home to the mother.

You making haste haste on decay: not blameworthy; life is good,
    be it stubbornly long or suddenly
A mortal splendor: meteors are not needed less than mountains:
    shine, perishing republic.

But for my children, I would have them keep their distance
    from the thickening center; corruption
Never has been compulsory, when the cities lie at the monster's
    feet there are left the mountains.

And boys, be in nothing so moderate as in love of man, a
    clever servant, insufferable master.
There is the trap that catches noblest spirits, that caught—they
    say—God, when he walked on earth.

CONTINENT'S END

At the equinox when the earth was veiled in a late rain,
    wreathed with wet poppies, waiting spring,
The ocean swelled for a far storm and beat its boundary, the
    ground-swell shook the beds of granite.

I gazing at the boundaries of granite and spray, the established
    sea-marks, felt behind me
Mountain and plain, the immense breadth of the continent,
    before me the mass and doubled stretch of water.

I said: You yoke the Aleutian seal-rocks with the lava and coral
    sowings that flower the south,
Over your flood the life that sought the sunrise faces ours that
    has followed the evening star.

The long migrations meet across you and it is nothing to you,
    you have forgotten us, mother.
You were much younger when we crawled out of the womb and
    lay in the sun's eye on the tideline.

It was long and long ago; we have grown proud since then and
    you have grown bitter; life retains
Your mobile soft unquiet strength; and envies hardness, the
    insolent quietness of stone.

The tides are in our veins, we still mirror the stars, life is your
child, but there is in me
Older and harder than life and more impartial, the eye that
watched before there was an ocean.

That watched you fill your beds out of the condensation of thin
vapor and watched you change them,
That saw you soft and violent wear your boundaries down, eat
rock, shift places with the continents.

Mother, though my song's measure is like your surf-beat's
ancient rhythm I never learned it of you.
Before there was any water there were tides of fire, both our
tones flow from the older fountain.

FROM

ROAN
STALLION

BIRDS

The fierce musical cries of a couple of sparrowhawks hunting on
the headland,
Hovering and darting, their heads northwestward,
Prick like silver arrows shot through a curtain the noise of the
ocean
Trampling its granite; their red backs gleam
Under my window around the stone corners; nothing
gracefuller, nothing
Nimbler in the wind. Westward the wave-gleaners,
The old gray sea-going gulls are gathered together, the
northwest wind wakening
Their wings to the wild spirals of the wind-dance.
Fresh as the air, salt as the foam, play birds in the bright wind,
fly falcons
Forgetting the oak and the pinewood, come gulls
From the Carmel sands and the sands at the river-mouth, from
Lobos and out of the limitless
Power of the mass of the sea, for a poem
Needs multitude, multitudes of thoughts, all fierce, all
flesh-eaters, musically clamorous
Bright hawks that hover and dart headlong, and ungainly
Gray hungers fledged with desire of transgression, salt slimed
beaks, from the sharp
Rock-shores of the world and the secret waters.

Sports and gallantries, the stage, the arts, the antics of dancers,
The exuberant voices of music,
Have charm for children but lack nobility; it is bitter
    earnestness
That makes beauty; the mind
Knows, grown adult.
                      A sudden fog-drift muffled the ocean,
A throbbing of engines moved in it,
At length, a stone's throw out, between the rocks and the
    vapor,
One by one moved shadows
Out of the mystery, shadows, fishing-boats, trailing each other
Following the cliff for guidance,
Holding a difficult path between the peril of the sea-fog
And the foam on the shore granite.
One by one, trailing their leader, six crept by me,
Out of the vapor and into it,
The throb of their engines subdued by the fog, patient and
    cautious,
Coasting all round the peninsula
Back to the buoys in Monterey harbor. A flight of pelicans
Is nothing lovelier to look at;
The flight of the planets is nothing nobler; all the arts lose
    virtue
Against the essential reality
Of creatures going about their business among the equally
Earnest elements of nature.

GRANITE AND CYPRESS

White-maned, wide-throated, the heavy-shouldered children of
    the wind leap at the sea-cliff.
The invisible falcon
Brooded on water and bred them in wide waste places, in a
    bride-chamber wide to the stars' eyes
In the center of the ocean,
Where no prows pass nor island is lifted . . . the sea beyond
    Lobos is whitened with the falcon's
Passage, he is here now,
The sky is one cloud, his wing-feathers hiss in the white grass,
    my sapling cypresses writhing
In the fury of his passage
Dare not dream of their centuries of future endurance of
    tempest. (I have granite and cypress,
Both long-lasting,
Planted in the earth; but the granite sea-boulders are prey to no
    hawk's wing, they have taken worse pounding,
Like me they remember
Old wars and are quiet; for we think that the future is one
    piece with the past, we wonder why tree-tops
And people are so shaken.)

Great-enough both accepts and subdues; the great frame takes
    all creatures;
From the greatness of their element they all take beauty.
Gulls; and the dingy freightship lurching south in the eye of a
    rain-wind;
The airplane dipping over the hill; hawks hovering
The white grass of the headland; cormorants roosting upon the
    guano-
Whitened skerries; pelicans awind; sea-slime
Shining at night in the wave-stir like drowned men's lanterns;
    smugglers signaling
A cargo to land; or the old Point Pinos lighthouse
Lawfully winking over dark water; the flight of the twilight
    herons,
Lonely wings and a cry; or with motor-vibrations
That hum in the rock like a new storm-tone of the ocean's to
    turn eyes westward
The navy's new-bought Zeppelin going by in the twilight,
Far out seaward; relative only to the evening star and the ocean
It slides into a cloud over Point Lobos.

A desert of weed and water-darkened stone under my western
   windows
The ebb lasted all afternoon,
And many pieces of humanity, men, women, and children,
   gathering shellfish,
Swarmed with voices of gulls the sea-breach.
At twilight they went off together, the verge was left vacant, an
   evening heron
Bent broad wings over the black ebb,
And left me wondering why a lone bird was dearer to me than
   many people.
Well: rare is dear: but also I suppose
Well reconciled with the world but not with our own natures
   we grudge to see them
Reflected on the world for a mirror.

AUTUMN EVENING

Though the little clouds ran southward still, the quiet autumnal
Cool of the late September evening
Seemed promising rain, rain, the change of the year, the angel
Of the sad forest. A heron flew over
With that remote ridiculous cry, "Quawk," the cry
That seems to make silence more silent. A dozen
Flops of the wing, a drooping glide, at the end of the glide
The cry, and a dozen flops of the wing.
I watched him pass on the autumn-colored sky; beyond him
Jupiter shone for evening star.
The sea's voice worked into my mood, I thought "No matter
What happens to men . . . the world's well made though."

THE TREASURE

Mountains, a moment's earth-waves rising and hollowing; the
   earth too's an ephemerid; the stars—
Short-lived as grass the stars quicken in the nebula and dry in
   their summer, they spiral
Blind up space, scattered black seeds of a future; nothing lives
   long, the whole sky's
Recurrences tick the seconds of the hours of the ages of the gulf
   before birth, and the gulf
After death is like dated: to labor eighty years in a notch of
   eternity is nothing too tiresome,
Enormous repose after, enormous repose before, the flash of
   activity.
Surely you never have dreamed the incredible depths were
   prologue and epilogue merely
To the surface play in the sun, the instant of life, what is called
   life? I fancy
That silence is the thing, this noise a found word for it;
   interjection, a jump of the breath at that silence;
Stars burn, grass grows, men breathe: as a man finding treasure
   says "Ah!" but the treasure's the essence;
Before the man spoke it was there, and after he has spoken he
   gathers it, inexhaustible treasure.

WOODROW WILSON

(FEBRUARY 1924)

It said "Come home, here is an end, a goal,
Not the one raced for, is it not better indeed? Victory you know
    requires
Force to sustain victory, the burden is never lightened, but final
    defeat
Buys peace: you have praised peace, peace without victory."

He said "It seems I am traveling no new way,
But leaving my great work unfinished how can I rest? I enjoyed
    a vision,
Endured betrayal, you must not ask me to endure final defeat,
Visionless men, blind hearts, blind mouths, live still."

It said "Yet perhaps your vision was less great
Than some you scorned, it has not proved even so practicable;
    Lenin
Enters this pass with less reluctance. As to betrayals: there are
    so many
Betrayals, the Russians and the Germans know."

He said "I knew I have enemies, I had not thought
To meet one at this brink: shall not the mocking voices die in
    the grave?"
It said "They shall. Soon there is silence." "I dreamed this
    end," he said, "when the prow
Of the long ship leaned against dawn, my people

Applauded me, and the world watched me. Again

I dreamed it at Versailles, the time I sent for the ship, and the
obstinate foreheads

That shared with me the settlement of the world flinched at my
threat and yielded.

That is all gone. . . . Do I remember this darkness?"

It said "No man forgets it but a moment.

The darkness before the mother, the depth of the return." "I
thought," he answered,

"That I was drawn out of this depth to establish the earth on
peace. My labor

Dies with me, why was I drawn out of this depth?"

It said "Loyal to your highest, sensitive, brave,

Sanguine, some few ways wise, you and all men are drawn out
of this depth

Only to be these things you are, as flowers for color, falcons for
swiftness,

Mountains for mass and quiet. Each for its quality

Is drawn out of this depth. Your tragic quality

Required the huge delusion of some major purpose to produce
it.

What, that the God of the stars needed your help?" He said
"This is my last

Worst pain, the bitter enlightenment that buys peace."

Man, introverted man, having crossed

In passage and but a little with the nature of things this latter
century

Has begot giants; but being taken up

Like a maniac with self-love and inward conflicts cannot manage
his hybrids.

Being used to deal with edgeless dreams,

Now he's bred knives on nature turns them also inward: they
have thirsty points though.

His mind forebodes his own destruction;

Actæon who saw the goddess naked among leaves and his
hounds tore him.

A little knowledge, a pebble from the shingle,

A drop from the oceans: who would have dreamed this
infinitely little too much?

ORESTES TO ELECTRA

FROM *THE TOWER BEYOND TRAGEDY*

ORESTES   I left the madness
    of the house, to-night in the dark, with you it walks yet.
How shall I tell you what I have learned? Your mind is like a
    hawk's or like a lion's, this knowledge
Is out of the order of your mind, a stranger language. To
    wild-beasts and the blood of kings
A verse blind in the book.

ELECTRA   At least my eyes can see dawn
    graying: tell and not mock me, our moment
Dies in a moment.

ORESTES   Here is the last labor
To spend on humanity. I saw a vision of us move in the dark:
    all that we did or dreamed of
Regarded each other, the man pursued the woman, the woman
    clung to the man, warriors and kings
Strained at each other in the darkness, all loved or fought
    inward, each one of the lost people
Sought the eyes of another that another should praise him;
    sought never his own but another's; the net of desire
Had every nerve drawn to the center, so that they writhed like a
    full draught of fishes, all matted
In the one mesh; when they look backward they see only a man
    standing at the beginning,
Or forward, a man at the end; or if upward, men in the shining
    bitter sky striding and feasting,

Whom you call Gods . . .

It is all turned inward, all your desires incestuous, the woman
    the serpent, the man the rose-red cavern,

Both human, worship forever . . .

ELECTRA   You have dreamed wretchedly.

ORESTES   I have
    seen the dreams of the people and not dreamed them.

As for me, I have slain my mother.

ELECTRA   No more?

ORESTES   And the gate's open,
    the gray boils over the mountain, I have greater

Kindred than dwell under a roof. Didn't I say this would be
    dark to you? I have cut the meshes

And fly like a freed falcon. To-night, lying on the hillside, sick
    with those visions, I remembered

The knife in the stalk of my humanity; I drew and it broke; I
    entered the life of the brown forest

And the great life of the ancient peaks, the patience of stone, I
    felt the changes in the veins

In the throat of the mountain, a grain in many centuries, we
    have our own time, not yours; and I was the stream

Draining the mountain wood; and I the stag drinking; and I was
    the stars,

Boiling with light, wandering alone, each one the lord of his
    own summit; and I was the darkness

Outside the stars, I included them, they were a part of me. I
    was mankind also, a moving lichen

On the cheek of the round stone . . . they have not made
    words for it, to go behind things, beyond hours and
    ages,

And be all things in all time, in their returns and passages, in
    the motionless and timeless center,
In the white of the fire . . . how can I express the excellence I
    have found, that has no color but clearness;
No honey but ecstasy; nothing wrought nor remembered; no
    undertone nor silver second murmur
That rings in love's voice, I and my loved are one; no desire but
    fulfilled; no passion but peace,
The pure flame and the white, fierier than any passion; no time
    but spheral eternity: Electra,
Was that your name before this life dawned—

ELECTRA   Here is mere death.
    Death like a triumph I'd have paid to keep you
A king in high Mycenæ: but here is shameful death, to die
    because I have lost you. They'll say
*Having done justice Agamemnon's son ran mad and was lost in the
    mountain; but Agamemnon's daughter*
*Hanged herself from a beam of the house: O bountiful hands of
    justice!* This horror draws upon me
Like stone walking.

ORESTES   What fills men's mouths is nothing; and your
    threat is nothing; I have fallen in love outward.
If I believed you—it is I that am like stone walking.

The dog barked; then the woman stood in the doorway, and
      hearing iron strike stone down the steep road
Covered her head with a black shawl and entered the light rain;
      she stood at the turn of the road.
A nobly formed woman; erect and strong as a new tower; the
      features stolid and dark
But sculptured into a strong grace; straight nose with a high
      bridge, firm and wide eyes, full chin,
Red lips; she was only a fourth part Indian; a Scottish sailor
      had planted her in young native earth,
Spanish and Indian, twenty-one years before. He had named her
      California when she was born;
That was her name; and had gone north.

                                    She heard the hooves
      and wheels come nearer, up the steep road.
The buckskin mare, leaning against the breastpiece, plodded
      into sight round the wet bank.
The pale face of the driver followed; the burnt-out eyes; they
      had fortune in them. He sat twisted
On the seat of the old buggy, leading a second horse by a long
      halter, a roan, a big one,
That stepped daintily; by the swell of the neck, a stallion.
     "What have you got, Johnny?" "Maskerel's stallion.
Mine now. I won him last night, I had very good luck." He was
      quite drunk. "They bring their mares up here now.
I keep this fellow. I got money besides, but I'll not show you."
     "Did you buy something, Johnny,

For our Christine? Christmas comes in two days, Johnny." "By
    God, forgot," he answered laughing.
"Don't tell Christine it's Christmas; after while I get her
    something, maybe." But California:
"I shared your luck when you lost: you lost *me* once, Johnny,
    remember? Tom Dell had me two nights
Here in the house: other times we've gone hungry: now that
    you've won, Christine will have her Christmas.
We share your luck, Johnny. You give me money, I go down to
    Monterey to-morrow,
Buy presents for Christine, come back in the evening. Next day
    Christmas." "You have wet ride," he answered
Giggling. "Here money. Five dollar; ten; twelve dollar. You buy
    two bottles of rye whiskey for Johnny."
"All right. I go to-morrow."

                                He was an outcast Hollander; not
    old, but shriveled with bad living.
The child Christine inherited from his race blue eyes, from his
    life a wizened forehead; she watched
From the house-door her father lurch out of the buggy and lead
    with due respect the stallion
To the new corral, the strong one; leaving the wearily breathing
    buckskin mare to his wife to unharness.

Storm in the night; the rain on the thin shakes of the roof like
    the ocean on rock streamed battering; once thunder
Walked down the narrow canyon into Carmel valley and wore
    away westward; Christine was wakeful
With fears and wonders; her father lay too deep for storm to
    touch him.

Dawn comes late in the year's dark,
Later into the crack of a canyon under redwoods; and
California slipped from bed
An hour before it; the buckskin would be tired; there was a
little barley, and why should Johnny
Feed all the barley to his stallion? That is what he would do.
She tip-toed out of the room.
Leaving her clothes, he'd waken if she waited to put them on,
and passed from the door of the house
Into the dark of the rain; the big black drops were cold through
the thin shift, but the wet earth
Pleasant under her naked feet. There was a pleasant smell in the
stable; and moving softly,
Touching things gently with the supple bend of the unclothed
body, was pleasant. She found a box,
Filled it with sweet dry barley and took it down to the old
corral. The little mare sighed deeply
At the rail in the wet darkness; and California returning
between two redwoods up to the house
Heard the happy jaws grinding the grain. Johnny could mind
the pigs and chickens. Christine called to her
When she entered the house, but slept again under her hand.
She laid the wet night-dress on a chair-back
And stole into the bedroom to get her clothes. A plank
creaked, and he wakened. She stood motionless
Hearing him stir in the bed. When he was quiet she stooped
after her shoes, and he said softly,
"What are you doing? Come back to bed." "It's late, I'm going
to Monterey, I must hitch up."

"You come to bed first. I been away three days. I give you
    money, I take back the money
And what you do in town then?" she sighed sharply and came
    to the bed.
            He reaching his hands from it
Felt the cool curve and firmness of her flank, and half rising
    caught her by the long wet hair.
She endured, and to hasten the act she feigned desire; she had
    not for long, except in dream, felt it.
Yesterday's drunkenness made him sluggish and exacting; she
    saw, turning her head sadly,
The windows were bright gray with dawn; he embraced her still,
    stopping to talk about the stallion.
At length she was permitted to put on her clothes. Clear
    daylight over the steep hills;
Gray-shining cloud over the tops of the redwoods; the winter
    stream sang loud; the wheels of the buggy
Slipped in deep slime, ground on washed stones at the road-edge.
    Down the hill the wrinkled river smothered the ford.
You must keep to the bed of stones: she knew the way by
    willow and alder: the buckskin halted mid-stream,
Shuddering, the water her own color washing up to the traces;
    but California, drawing up
Her feet out of the whirl onto the seat of the buggy swung the
    whip over the yellow water
And drove to the road.
                    All morning the clouds were racing
    northward like a river. At noon they thickened.
When California faced the southwind home from Monterey it
    was heavy with level rainfall.

She looked seaward from the foot of the valley; red rays cried
    sunset from a trumpet of streaming
Cloud over Lobos, the southwest occident of the solstice.
    Twilight came soon, but the tired mare
Feared the road more than the whip. Mile after mile of slow
    gray twilight.
                Then, quite suddenly, darkness.
"Christine will be asleep. It is Christmas Eve. The ford. That
    hour of daylight wasted this morning!"
She could see nothing; she let the reins lie on the dashboard
    and knew at length by the cramp of the wheels
And the pitch down, they had reached it. Noise of wheels on
    stones, plashing of hooves in water; a world
Of sounds; no sight; the gentle thunder of water; the mare
    snorting, dipping her head, one knew,
To look for footing, in the blackness, under the stream. The
    hushing and creaking of the sea-wind
In the passion of invisible willows.
                     The mare stood still; the
    woman shouted to her; spared whip,
For a false leap would lose the track of the ford. She stood.
    "The baby's things," thought California,
"Under the seat: the water will come over the floor"; and rising
    in the midst of the water
She tilted the seat; fetched up the doll, the painted wooden
    chickens, the woolly bear, the book
Of many pictures, the box of sweets: she brought them all from
    under the seat and stored them, trembling,
Under her clothes, about the breasts, under the arms; the
    corners of the cardboard boxes

Cut into the soft flesh; but with a piece of rope for a girdle and
　　wound about the shoulders
All was made fast. The mare stood still as if asleep in the midst
　　of the water. Then California
Reached out a hand over the stream and fingered her rump; the
　　solid wet convexity of it
Shook like the beat of a great heart. "What are you waiting
　　for?" But the feel of the animal surface
Had wakened a dream, obscured real danger with a dream of
　　danger. "What for? For the water-stallion
To break out of the stream, that is what the rump strains for,
　　him to come up flinging foam sidewise,
Fore-hooves in air, crush me and the rig and curl over his
　　woman." She flung out with the whip then,
The mare plunged forward. The buggy drifted sidelong: was she
　　off ground? Swimming? No: by the splashes.
The driver, a mere prehensile instinct, clung to the side-irons of
　　the seat and felt the force
But not the coldness of the water, curling over her knees,
　　breaking up to the waist
Over her body. They'd turned. The mare had turned up stream
　　and was wallowing back into shoal water.
Then California dropped her forehead to her knees, having seen
　　nothing, feeling a danger,
And felt the brute weight of a branch of alder, the pendulous
　　light leaves brush her bent neck
Like a child's fingers. The mare burst out of water and
　　stopped on the slope to the ford. The woman climbed
　　down

Between the wheels and went to her head. "Poor Dora," she
    called her by her name, "there, Dora. Quietly,"
And led her around, there was room to turn on the margin, the
    head to the gentle thunder of the water.
She crawled on hands and knees, felt for the ruts, and shifted
    the wheels into them. "You can see, Dora.
I can't. But this time you'll go through it." She climbed into the
    seat and shouted angrily. The mare
Stopped, her two forefeet in the water. She touched with the
    whip. The mare plodded ahead and halted.
Then California thought of prayer: "Dear little Jesus,
Dear baby Jesus born to-night, your head was shining
Like silver candles. I've got a baby too, only a girl. You had
    light wherever you walked.
Dear baby Jesus give me light." Light streamed: rose, gold, rich
    purple, hiding the ford like a curtain.
The gentle thunder of water was a noise of wing-feathers, the
    fans of paradise lifting softly.
The child afloat on radiance had a baby face, but the angels
    had birds' heads, hawks' heads,
Bending over the baby, weaving a web of wings about him. He
    held in the small fat hand
A little snake with golden eyes, and California could see clearly
    on the under radiance
The mare's pricked ears, a sharp black fork against the shining
    light-fall. But it dropped; the light of heaven
Frightened poor Dora. She backed; swung up the water,
And nearly oversetting the buggy turned and scrambled
    backward; the iron wheel-tires rang on boulders.

*   *   *

Then California weeping climbed between the wheels. Her wet
    clothes and the toys packed under
Dragged her down with their weight; she stripped off cloak and
    dress and laid the baby's things in the buggy;
Brought Johnny's whiskey out from under the seat; wrapped all
    in the dress, bottles and toys, and tied them
Into a bundle that would sling over her back. She unharnessed
    the mare, hurting her fingers
Against the swollen straps and the wet buckles. She tied the
    pack over her shoulders, the cords
Crossing her breasts, and mounted. She drew up her shift about
    her waist and knotted it, naked thighs
Clutching the sides of the mare, bare flesh to the wet withers,
    and caught the mane with her right hand,
The looped-up bridle-reins in the other. "Dora, the baby gives
    you light." The blinding radiance
Hovered the ford. "Sweet baby Jesus give us light." Cataracts of
    light and Latin singing
Fell through the willows; the mare snorted and reared: the roar
    and thunder of the invisible water;
The night shaking open like a flag, shot with the flashes; the
    baby face hovering; the water
Beating over her shoes and stockings up to the bare thighs; and
    over them, like a beast
Lapping her belly; the wriggle and pitch of the mare swimming;
    the drift, the sucking water; the blinding
Light above and behind with not a gleam before, in the throat
    of darkness; the shock of the fore-hooves
Striking bottom, the struggle and surging lift of the haunches.
    She felt the water streaming off her

From the shoulders down; heard the great strain and sob of the
    mare's breathing, heard the horseshoes grind on gravel.
When California came home the dog at the door snuffed at her
    without barking; Christine and Johnny
Both were asleep; she did not sleep for hours, but kindled fire
    and knelt patiently over it,
Shaping and drying the dear-bought gifts for Christmas
    morning.

She hated (she thought) the proud-necked stallion.
He'd lean the big twin masses of his breast on the rail, his
    red-brown eyes flash the white crescents,
She admired him then, she hated him for his uselessness,
    serving nothing
But Johnny's vanity. Horses were too cheap to breed. She
    thought, if he could range in freedom,
Shaking the red-roan mane for a flag on the bare hills.
                                  A man
    brought up a mare in April;
Then California, though she wanted to watch, stayed with
    Christine indoors. When the child fretted
The mother told her once more about the miracle of the ford;
    her prayer to the little Jesus
The Christmas Eve when she was bringing the gifts home; the
    appearance, the lights, the Latin singing,
The thunder of wing-feathers and water, the shining child, the
    cataracts of splendor down the darkness.
"A little baby," Christine asked, "the God is a baby?" "The
    child of God. That was his birthday.
His mother was named Mary: we pray to her too: God came to
    her. He was not the child of a man

Like you or me. God was his father: she was the stallion's
    wife—what did I say—God's wife,"
She said with a cry, lifting Christine aside, pacing the planks of
    the floor. "She is called more blessed
Than any woman. She was so good, she was more loved." "Did
    God live near her house?" "He lives
Up high, over the stars; he ranges on the bare blue hill of the
    sky." In her mind a picture
Flashed, of the red-roan mane shaken out for a flag on the bare
    hills, and she said quickly, "He's more
Like a great man holding the sun in his hand." Her mind giving
    her words the lie, "But no one
Knows, only the shining and the power. The power, the terror,
    the burning fire covered her over . . ."
"Was she burnt up, mother?" "She was so good and lovely, she
    was the mother of the little Jesus.
If you are good nothing will hurt you." "What did she think?"
    "She loved, she was not afraid of the hooves—
Hands that had made the hills and sun and moon, and the sea
    and the great redwoods, the terrible strength,
She gave herself without thinking." "You only saw the baby,
    mother?" "Yes, and the angels about him,
The great wild shining over the black river." Three times she
    had walked to the door, three times returned,
And now the hand that had thrice hung on the knob, full of
    prevented action, twisted the cloth
Of the child's dress that she had been mending. "Oh, oh, I've
    torn it." She struck at the child and then embraced her
Fiercely, the small blonde sickly body.

                        Johnny came in, his face
    reddened as if he had stood

Near fire, his eyes triumphing. "Finished," he said, and looked
    with malice at Christine. "I go
Down valley with Jim Carrier; owes me five dollar, fifteen I
    charge him, he brought ten in his pocket.
Has grapes on the ranch, maybe I take a barrel red wine instead
    of money. Be back to-morrow.
To-morrow night I tell you—Eh, Jim," he laughed over his
    shoulder, "I say to-morrow evening
I show her how the red fellow act, the big fellow. When I come
    home." She answered nothing, but stood
In front of the door, holding the little hand of her daughter, in
    the path of sun between the redwoods,
While Johnny tied the buckskin mare behind Carrier's buggy,
    and bringing saddle and bridle tossed them
Under the seat. Jim Carrier's mare, the bay, stood with drooped
    head and started slowly, the men
Laughing and shouting at her; their voices could be heard down
    the steep road, after the noise
Of the iron-hooped wheels died from the stone. Then one
    might hear the hush of the wind in the tall redwoods,
The tinkle of the April brook, deep in its hollow.

                                        Humanity is
    the start of the race; I say
Humanity is the mould to break away from, the crust to break
    through, the coal to break into fire,
The atom to be split.
                        Tragedy that breaks man's face and a
    white fire flies out of it; vision that fools him
Out of his limits, desire that fools him out of his limits,
    unnatural crime, inhuman science,

Slit eyes in the mask; wild loves that leap over the walls of
    nature, the wild fence-vaulter science,
Useless intelligence of far stars, dim knowledge of the spinning
    demons that make an atom,
These break, these pierce, these deify, praising their God shrilly
    with fierce voices: not in a man's shape
He approves the praise, he that walks lightning-naked on the
    Pacific, that laces the suns with planets,
The heart of the atom with electrons: what is humanity in this
    cosmos? For him, the last
Least taint of a trace in the dregs of the solution; for itself, the
    mould to break away from, the coal
To break into fire, the atom to be split.

                                        After the child slept,
        after the leopard-footed evening
Had glided oceanward, California turned the lamp to its least
    flame and glided from the house.
She moved sighing, like a loose fire, backward and forward on
    the smooth ground by the door.
She heard the night-wind that draws down the valley like the
    draught in a flue under clear weather
Whisper and toss in the tall redwoods; she heard the tinkle of
    the April brook deep in its hollow.
Cooled by the night the odors that the horses had left behind
    were in her nostrils; the night
Whitened up the bare hill; a drift of coyotes by the river cried
    bitterly against moonrise;
Then California ran to the old corral, the empty one where
    they kept the buckskin mare,

And leaned, and bruised her breasts on the rail, feeling the sky
    whiten. When the moon stood over the hill
She stole to the house. The child breathed quietly. Herself: to
    sleep? She had seen Christ in the night at Christmas.
The hills were shining open to the enormous night of the April
    moon: empty and empty,
The vast round backs of the bare hills? If one should ride up
    high might not the Father himself
Be seen brooding His night, cross-legged, chin in hand,
    squatting on the last dome? More likely
Leaping the hills, shaking the red-roan mane for a flag on the
    bare hills. She blew out the lamp.
Every fiber of flesh trembled with faintness when she came to
    the door; strength lacked, to wander
Afoot into the shining of the hill, high enough, high enough
    . . . the hateful face of a man had taken
The strength that might have served her, the corral was empty.
    The dog followed her, she caught him by the collar,
Dragged him in fierce silence back to the door of the house,
    latched him inside.
It was like daylight
Outdoors and she hastened without faltering down the
    footpath, through the dark fringe of twisted oak-brush,
To the open place in a bay of the hill. The dark strength of the
    stallion had heard her coming; she heard him
Blow the shining air out of his nostrils, she saw him in the
    white lake of moonlight
Move like a lion along the timbers of the fence, shaking the
    nightfall
Of the great mane; his fragrance came to her; she leaned on the
    fence;

He drew away from it, the hooves making soft thunder in the
    trodden soil.
Wild love had trodden it, his wrestling with the stranger, the
    shame of the day
Had stamped it into mire and powder when the heavy fetlocks
Strained the soft flanks. "Oh, if I could bear you!
If I had the strength. O great God that came down to Mary,
    gently you came. But I will ride him
Up into the hill, if he throws me, if he tramples me, is it not
    my desire
To endure death?" She climbed the fence, pressing her body
    against the rail, shaking like fever,
And dropped inside to the soft ground. He neither threatened
    her with his teeth nor fled from her coming,
And lifting her hand gently to the upflung head she caught the
    strap of the headstall,
That hung under the quivering chin. She unlooped the halter
    from the high strength of the neck
And the arch the storm-cloud mane hung with live darkness.
    He stood; she crushed her breasts
On the hard shoulder, an arm over the withers, the other under
    the mass of his throat, and murmuring
Like a mountain dove, "If I could bear you." No way, no help,
    a gulf in nature. She murmured, "Come,
We will run on the hill. O beautiful, O beautiful," and led him
To the gate and flung the bars on the ground. He threw his
    head downward
To snuff at the bars; and while he stood, she catching mane and
    withers with all sudden contracture

And strength of her lithe body, leaped, clung hard, and was
    mounted. He had been ridden before; he did not
Fight the weight but ran like a stone falling;
Broke down the slope into the moon-glass of the stream, and
    flattened to his neck
She felt the branches of a buckeye tree fly over her, saw the
    wall of the oak-scrub
End her world: but he turned there, the matted branches
Scraped her right knee, the great slant shoulders
Laboring the hill-slope, up, up, the clear hill. Desire had died in
    her
At the first rush, the falling like death, but now it revived,
She feeling between her thighs the labor of the great engine, the
    running muscles, the hard swiftness,
She riding the savage and exultant strength of the world.
    Having topped the thicket he turned eastward,
Running less wildly; and now at length he felt the halter when
    she drew on it; she guided him upward;
He stopped and grazed on the great arch and pride of the hill,
    the silent calvary. A dwarfish oakwood
Climbed the other slope out of the dark of the unknown
    canyon beyond; the last wind-beaten bush of it
Crawled up to the height, and California slipping from her
    mount tethered him to it. She stood then,
Shaking. Enormous films of moonlight
Trailed down from the height. Space, anxious whiteness,
    vastness. Distant beyond conception the shining
    ocean
Lay light like a haze along the ledge and doubtful world's end.
    Little vapors gleaming, and little

Darknesses on the far chart underfoot symbolized wood and
	valley; but the air was the element, the moon-
Saturate arcs and spires of the air.
									Here is solitude, here on the
	calvary, nothing conscious
But the possible God and the cropped grass, no witness, no eye
	but that misformed one, the moon's past fullness.
Two figures on the shining hill, woman and stallion, she
	kneeling to him, brokenly adoring.
He cropping the grass, shifting his hooves, or lifting the long
	head to gaze over the world,
Tranquil and powerful. She prayed aloud, "O God, I am not
	good enough, O fear, O strength, I am draggled.
Johnny and other men have had me, and O clean power! Here
	am I," she said, falling before him,
And crawled to his hooves. She lay a long while, as if asleep, in
	reach of the fore-hooves, weeping. He avoided
Her head and the prone body. He backed at first; but later
	plucked the grass that grew by her shoulder.
The small dark head under his nostrils: a small round stone,
	that smelt human, black hair growing from it:
The skull shut the light in: it was not possible for any eyes
To know what throbbed and shone under the sutures of the
	skull, or a shell full of lightning
Had scared the roan strength, and he'd have broken tether,
	screaming, and run for the valley.
									The atom bounds-breaking,
Nucleus to sun, electrons to planets, with recognition
Not praying, self-equaling, the whole to the whole, the
	microcosm

Not entering nor accepting entrance, more equally, more utterly,
more incredibly conjugate
With the other extreme and greatness; passionately perceptive of
identity. . . .
The fire threw up figures
And symbols meanwhile, racial myths formed and dissolved in
it, the phantom rulers of humanity
That without being are yet more real than what they are born
of, and without shape, shape that which makes them:
The nerves and the flesh go by shadowlike, the limbs and the
lives shadowlike, these shadows remain, these shadows
To whom temples, to whom churches, to whom labors and
wars, visions and dreams are dedicate:
Out of the fire in the small round stone that black moss
covered, a crucified man writhed up in anguish;
A woman covered by a huge beast in whose mane the stars were
netted, sun and moon were his eyeballs,
Smiled under the unendurable violation, her throat swollen with
the storm and blood-flecks gleaming
On the stretched lips; a woman—no, a dark water, split by jets
of lightning, and after a season
What floated up out of the furrowed water, a boat, a fish, a
fire-globe?
It had wings, the creature,
And flew against the fountain of lightning, fell burnt out of the
cloud back to the bottomless water . . .
Figures and symbols, castlings of the fire, played in her brain;
but the white fire was the essence,
The burning in the small round shell of bone that black hair
covered, that lay by the hooves on the hilltop.

She rose at length, she unknotted the halter; she walked and led
    the stallion; two figures, woman and stallion,
Came down the silent emptiness of the dome of the hill, under
    the cataract of the moonlight.

The next night there was moon through cloud. Johnny had
    returned half drunk toward evening, and California
Who had known him for years with neither love nor loathing
    to-night hating him had let the child Christine
Play in the light of the lamp for hours after her bedtime; who
    fell asleep at length on the floor
Beside the dog; then Johnny: "Put her to bed." She gathered
    the child against her breasts, she laid her
In the next room, and covered her with a blanket. The window
    was white, the moon had risen. The mother
Lay down by the child, but after a moment Johnny stood in the
    doorway. "Come drink." He had brought home
Two jugs of wine slung from the saddle, part payment for the
    stallion's service; a pitcher of it
Was on the table, and California sadly came and emptied her
    glass. Whiskey, she thought,
Would have erased him till to-morrow; the thin red wine. . . .
    "We have a good evening," he laughed, pouring it.
"One glass yet then I show you what the red fellow did." She
    moving toward the house-door his eyes
Followed her, the glass filled and the red juice ran over the
    table. When it struck the floor-planks
He heard and looked. "Who stuck the pig?" he muttered
    stupidly, "here's blood, here's blood," and trailed his
    fingers

In the red lake under the lamplight. While he was looking down
    the door creaked, she had slipped outdoors,
And he, his mouth curving like a faun's imagined the chase
    under the solemn redwoods, the panting
And unresistant victim caught in a dark corner. He emptied the
    glass and went outdoors
Into the dappled lanes of moonlight. No sound but the April
    brook's. "Hey Bruno," he called, "find her.
Bruno, go find her." The dog after a little understood and
    quested, the man following.
When California crouching by an oak-bush above the house
    heard them come near she darted
To the open slope and ran down hill. The dog barked at her
    heels, pleased with the game, and Johnny
Followed in silence. She ran down to the new corral, she saw
    the stallion
Move like a lion along the timbers of the fence, the dark arched
    neck shaking the nightfall
Of the great mane; she threw herself prone and writhed under
    the bars, his hooves backing away from her
Made muffled thunder in the soft soil. She stood in the midst of
    the corral, panting, but Johnny
Paused at the fence. The dog ran under it, and seeing the
    stallion move, the woman standing quiet,
Danced after the beast, with white-tooth feints and dashes.
    When Johnny saw the formidable dark strength
Recoil from the dog, he climbed up over the fence.
The child Christine waked when her mother left her
And lay half dreaming, in the half-waking dream she saw the
    ocean come up out of the west

And cover the world, she looked up through clear water at the
    tops of the redwoods. She heard the door creak
And the house empty; her heart shook her body, sitting up on
    the bed, and she heard the dog
And crept toward light, where it gleamed under the crack of the
    door. She opened the door, the room was empty,
The table-top was a red lake under the lamplight. The color of
    it was terrible to her;
She had seen the red juice drip from a coyote's muzzle her
    father had shot one day in the hills
And carried him home over the saddle: she looked at the rifle
    on the wall-rack: it was not moved:
She ran to the door, the dog was barking and the moon was
    shining: she knew wine by the odor
But the color frightened her, the empty house frightened her,
    she followed down hill in the white lane of moonlight
The friendly noise of the dog. She saw in the big horse's corral,
    on the level shoulder of the hill,
Black on white, the dark strength of the beast, the dancing fury
    of the dog, and the two others.
One fled, one followed; the big one charged, rearing; one fell
    under his fore-hooves. She heard her mother
Scream: without thought she ran to the house, she dragged a
    chair past the red pool and climbed to the rifle,
Got it down from the wall and lugged it somehow through the
    door and down the hillside, under the hard weight
Sobbing. Her mother stood by the rails of the corral, she gave it
    to her. On the far side
The dog flashed at the plunging stallion; in the midst of the
    space the man, slow-moving, like a hurt worm

Crawling, dragged his body by inches toward the fence-line.
　　Then California, resting the rifle
On the top rail, without doubting, without hesitance,
Aimed for the leaping body of the dog, and when it stood,
　　fired. It snapped, rolled over, lay quiet.
"O mother you've hit Bruno!" "I couldn't see the sights in the
　　moonlight," she answered quietly. She stood
And watched, resting the rifle-butt on the ground. The stallion
　　wheeled, freed from his torment, the man
Lurched up to his knees, wailing a thin and bitter bird's cry,
　　and the roan thunder
Struck; hooves left nothing alive but teeth tore up the remnant.
　　"O mother, shoot, shoot!" Yet California
Stood carefully watching, till the beast having fed all his fury
　　stretched neck to utmost, head high,
And wrinkled back the upper lip from the teeth, yawning
　　obscene disgust over—not a man—
A smear on the moon-like earth: then California moved by
　　some obscure human fidelity
Lifted the rifle. Each separate nerve-cell of her brain flaming the
　　stars fell from their places
Crying in her mind: she fired three times before the haunches
　　crumpled sidewise, the forelegs stiffening,
And the beautiful strength settled to earth: she turned then on
　　her little daughter the mask of a woman
Who has killed God. The night-wind veering, the smell of the
　　spilt wine drifted down hill from the house.

FROM

*AN AMERICAN
MISCELLANY*

APOLOGY FOR BAD DREAMS

I

In the purple light, heavy with redwood, the slopes drop
    seaward,
Headlong convexities of forest, drawn in together to the steep
    ravine. Below, on the sea-cliff,
A lonely clearing; a little field of corn by the streamside; a roof
    under spared trees. Then the ocean
Like a great stone someone has cut to a sharp edge and
    polished to shining. Beyond it, the fountain
And furnace of incredible light flowing up from the sunk sun.
    In the little clearing a woman
Is punishing a horse; she had tied the halter to a sapling at the
    edge of the wood, but when the great whip
Clung to the flanks the creature kicked so hard she feared he
    would snap the halter; she called from the house
The young man her son; who fetched a chain tie-rope, they
    working together
Noosed the small rusty links round the horse's tongue
And tied him by the swollen tongue to the tree.
Seen from this height they are shrunk to insect size.
Out of all human relation. You cannot distinguish
The blood dripping from where the chain is fastened,
The beast shuddering; but the thrust neck and the legs
Far apart. You can see the whip fall on the flanks . . .
The gesture of the arm. You cannot see the face of the woman.
The enormous light beats up out of the west across the
    cloud-bars of the trade-wind. The ocean

Darkens, the high clouds brighten, the hills darken together.
    Unbridled and unbelievable beauty
Covers the evening world . . . not covers, grows apparent out of
    it, as Venus down there grows out
From the lit sky. What said the prophet? "I create good: and I
    create evil: I am the Lord."

II

This coast crying out for tragedy like all beautiful places,
(The quiet ones ask for quieter suffering: but here the granite
    cliff the gaunt cypresses crown
Demands what victim? The dykes of red lava and black what
    Titan? The hills like pointed flames
Beyond Soberanes, the terrible peaks of the bare hills under the
    sun, what immolation?)
This coast crying out for tragedy like all beautiful places: and
    like the passionate spirit of humanity
Pain for its bread: God's, many victims', the painful deaths, the
    horrible transfigurements: I said in my heart,
"Better invent than suffer: imagine victims
Lest your own flesh be chosen the agonist, or you
Martyr some creature to the beauty of the place." And I said,
"Burn sacrifices once a year to magic
Horror away from the house, this little house here
You have built over the ocean with your own hands
Beside the standing boulders: for what are we,
The beast that walks upright, with speaking lips
And little hair, to think we should always be fed,
Sheltered, intact, and self-controlled? We sooner more liable
Than the other animals. Pain and terror, the insanities of desire;
    not accidents but essential,

And crowd up from the core:" I imagined victims for those
　　wolves, I made them phantoms to follow,
They have hunted the phantoms and missed the house. It is not
　　good to forget over what gulfs the spirit
Of the beauty of humanity, the petal of a lost flower blown
　　seaward by the night-wind, floats to its quietness.

III

Boulders blunted like an old bear's teeth break up from the
　　headland; below them
All the soil is thick with shells, the tide-rock feasts of a dead
　　people.
Here the granite flanks are scarred with ancient fire, the ghosts
　　of the tribe
Crouch in the nights beside the ghost of a fire, they try to
　　remember the sunlight,
Light has died out of their skies. These have paid something for
　　the future
Luck of the country, while we living keep old griefs in memory:
　　though God's
Envy is not a likely fountain of ruin, to forget evils calls down
Sudden reminders from the cloud: remembered deaths be our
　　redeemers;
Imagined victims our salvation: white as the half moon at
　　midnight
Someone flamelike passed me, saying, "I am Tamar Cauldwell, I
　　have my desire,"
Then the voice of the sea returned, when she had gone by, the
　　stars to their towers.
. . . Beautiful country burn again, Point Pinos down to the Sur
　　Rivers

Burn as before with bitter wonders, land and ocean and the
Carmel water.

IV

He brays humanity in a mortar to bring the savor
From the bruised root: a man having bad dreams, who invents
victims, is only the ape of that God.
He washes it out with tears and many waters, calcines it with
fire in the red crucible,
Deforms it, makes it horrible to itself: the spirit flies out and
stands naked, he sees the spirit,
He takes it in the naked ecstasy; it breaks in his hand, the atom
is broken, the power that massed it
Cries to the power that moves the stars, "I have come home to
myself, behold me.
I bruised myself in the flint mortar and burnt me
In the red shell, I tortured myself, I flew forth,
Stood naked of myself and broke me in fragments,
And here am I moving the stars that are me."
I have seen these ways of God: I know of no reason
For fire and change and torture and the old returnings.
He being sufficient might be still. I think they admit no reason;
they are the ways of my love.
Unmeasured power, incredible passion, enormous craft: no
thought apparent but burns darkly
Smothered with its own smoke in the human brain-vault: no
thought outside: a certain measure in phenomena:
The fountains of the boiling stars, the flowers on the foreland,
the ever-returning roses of dawn.

ANTE MORTEM

It is likely enough that lions and scorpions
Guard the end; life never was bonded to be endurable nor the
    act of dying
Unpainful; the brain burning too often
Earns, though it held itself detached from the object, often a
    burnt age.
No matter, I shall not shorten it by hand.
Incapable of body or unmoved of brain is no evil, one always
    went envying
The quietness of stones. But if the striped blossom
Insanity spread lewd splendors and lightning terrors at the end
    of the forest;
Or intolerable pain work its known miracle,
Exile the monarch soul, set a sick monkey in the office . . .
    remember me
Entire and balanced when I was younger,
And could lift stones, and comprehend in the praises the
    cruelties of life.

Happy people die whole, they are all dissolved in a moment,
    they have had what they wanted,
No hard gifts; the unhappy
Linger a space, but pain is a thing that is glad to be forgotten;
    but one who has given
His heart to a cause or a country,
His ghost may spaniel it a while, disconsolate to watch it. I was
    wondering how long the spirit
That sheds this verse will remain
When the nostrils are nipped, when the brain rots in its vault
    or bubbles in the violence of fire
To be ash in metal. I was thinking
Some stalks of the wood whose roots I married to the earth of
    this place will stand five centuries;
I held the roots in my hand,
The stems of the trees between two fingers: how many remote
    generations of women
Will drink joy from men's loins,
And dragged from between the thighs of what mothers will
    giggle at my ghost when it curses the axemen,
Gray impotent voice on the sea-wind,
When the last trunk falls? The women's abundance will have
    built roofs over all this foreland;
Will have buried the rock foundations
I laid here: the women's exuberance will canker and fail in its
    time and like clouds the houses
Unframe, the granite of the prime

Stand from the heaps: come storm and wash clean: the plaster
    is all run to the sea and the steel
All rusted; the foreland resumes
The form we loved when we saw it. Though one at the end of
    the age and far off from this place
Should meet my presence in a poem,
The ghost would not care but be here, long sunset shadow in
    the seams of the granite, and forgotten
The flesh, a spirit for the stone.

LOVE CHILDREN

The trail's high up on the ridge, no one goes down
But the east wind and the falling water the concave slope
        without a name to the little bay
That has no name either. The fish-hawk plunges
Beyond the long rocks, rises with streaming silver; the eagle
        strikes down from the ridge and robs the fish-hawk.
The stunted redwoods neither grow nor grow old
Up the steep slope, remembering winter and the sea-wind; the
        ferns are maiden green by the falling water;
The seas whiten on the reefs; nothing has changed
For a thousand years, ten thousand. It is not a thousand, it is
        only seventy, since man and woman came down
The untrampled slope, forcing a trail through lupine
And mountain laurel; they built a hut against the stream-side;
        the coast cannot remember their names.
They had light eyes and white skins, and nobody knew
What they fled, why they came. They had children in this place;
        loved while they clung to the breast but later
Naked, untaught, uncared for, as wild as foxes,
A boy and a girl; the coast remembers they would squat beside
        a squirrel's earth until the furred thing
Crept out, then what the small hands caught the teeth
Would tear living. What implacable flame of passion I wonder
        left its children forgotten
To eat vermin and the raw mussels of the rock?
Love at the height is a bad hearth-fire, a wolf in the house to
        keep the children. I imagine languors,

Sick loathing, miserable renewals, blind insolence
In the eye of the noon sun. They'd stripped to bathe, desire on
    the salted beach between the skerries
Came bronze-clawed like a hawk; the children to see
Was the deep pearl, the last abandonment. They lived twelve
    years in the hut beside the stream, and the children
Died, and the hut is fallen and vanished, the paths
Filled with thicket and vanished utterly. Nothing remains.
    Certainly a flame burned in this place;
Its lamps wandered away, no one knows whither.
The flaming oil-drops fell and burned out. No one imagines that
    ghosts move here, at noon or at midnight.
I'm never sorry to think that here's a planet
Will go on like this glen, perfectly whole and content, after
    mankind is scummed from the kettle.
No ghost will walk under the latter starlight.
The little phials of desire have all been emptied and broken.
    Here the ocean echoes, the stream's like bird-song;
The stunted redwoods neither grow nor grow old
Up the steep slope, remembering winter and the sea-wind; the
    ferns are maiden green by the falling water;
The seas whiten on the reefs; the fish-hawk plunges
Beyond the long rocks, rises with streaming silver; the eagle
    strikes down from the ridge and robs the fish-hawk.

Enormous cloud-mountains that form over Point Lobos and into
    the sunset,
Figures of fire on the walls of to-night's storm,
Foam of gold in gorges of fire, and the great file of warrior
    angels:
Dreams gathering in the curded brain of the earth,
The sky the brain-vault, on the threshold of sleep: poor earth,
    you like your children
By inordinate desires tortured make dreams?
Storms more enormous, wars nobler, more toppling mountains,
    more jewelled waters, more free
Fires on impossible headlands . . . as a poor girl
Wishing her lover taller and more desirous, and herself maned
    with gold,
Dreams the world right, in the cold bed, about dawn.
Dreams are beautiful; the slaves of form are beautiful also; I
    have grown to believe
A stone is a better pillow than many visions.

OCTOBER EVENING

Male-throated under the shallow sea-fog
Moaned a ship's horn quivering the shorelong granite.
Coyotes toward the valley made answer,
Their little wolf-pads in the dead grass by the stream
Wet with the young season's first rain,
Their jagged wail trespassing among the steep stars.
What stars? Aldebaran under the dove-leash
Pleiades. I thought, in an hour Orion will be risen,
Be glad for summer is dead and the sky
Turns over to darkness, good storms, few guests, glad rivers.

PELICANS

Four pelicans went over the house,
Sculled their worn oars over the courtyard: I saw that
    ungainliness
Magnifies the idea of strength.
A lifting gale of sea-gulls followed them; slim yachts of the
    element,
Natural growths of the sky, no wonder
Light wings to leave sea; but those grave weights toil, and are
    powerful,
And the wings torn with old storms remember
The cone that the oldest redwood dropped from, the tilting of
    continents,
The dinosaur's day, the lift of new sea-lines.
The omnisecular spirit keeps the old with the new also.
Nothing at all has suffered erasure.
There is life not of our time. He calls ungainly bodies
As beautiful as the grace of horses.
He is weary of nothing; he watches air-planes; he watches
    pelicans.

 CREDO

My friend from Asia has powers and magic, he plucks a blue
    leaf from the young blue-gum
And gazing upon it, gathering and quieting
The God in his mind, creates an ocean more real than the
    ocean, the salt, the actual
Appalling presence, the power of the waters.
He believes that nothing is real except as we make it. I humbler
    have found in my blood
Bred west of Caucasus a harder mysticism.
Multitude stands in my mind but I think that the ocean in the
    bone vault is only
The bone vault's ocean: out there is the ocean's;
The water is the water, the cliff is the rock, come shocks and
    flashes of reality. The mind
Passes, the eye closes, the spirit is a passage;
The beauty of things was born before eyes and sufficient to
    itself; the heart-breaking beauty
Will remain when there is no heart to break for it.

FROM

THE WOMEN
AT POINT SUR

 PRELUDE

I drew solitude
           over me, on the lone shore,
By the hawk-perch stones; the hawks and the gulls are never
           breakers of solitude.
When the animals Christ was rumored to have died for drew in,
The land thickening, drew in about me, I planted trees
           eastward, and the ocean
Secured the west with the quietness of thunder. I was quiet.
Imagination, the traitor of the mind, has taken my solitude and
           slain it.
No peace but many companions; the hateful-eyed
And human-bodied are all about me: you that love multitude
           may have them.

But why should I make fables again? There are many
Tellers of tales to delight women and the people.
I have no vocation. The old rock under the house, the hills
           with their hard roots and the ocean hearted
With sacred quietness from here to Asia
Make me ashamed to speak of the active little bodies, the
           coupling bodies, the misty brainfuls
Of perplexed passion. Humanity is needless.
I said, "Humanity is the start of the race, the gate to break
           away from, the coal to kindle,
The blind mask crying to be slit with eye-holes."
Well, now it is done, the mask slit, the rag burnt, the
           starting-post left behind: but not in a fable.

Culture's outlived, art's root-cut, discovery's

The way to walk in. Only remains to invent the language to tell

    it. Match-ends of burnt experience

Human enough to be understood,

Scraps and metaphors will serve. The wine was a little too

    strong for the new wine-skins . . .

                       Come storm, kind storm.

Summer and the days of tired gold

And bitter blue are more ruinous.

The leprous grass, the sick forest,

The sea like a whore's eyes,

And the noise of the sun,

The yellow dog barking in the blue pasture,

Snapping sidewise.

            When I remembered old rains,

Running clouds and the iron wind, then the trees trembled.

I was calling one of the great dancers

Who wander down from the Aleutian rocks and the open

    Pacific,

Pivoting counter-sunwise, celebrating power with the whirl of a

    dance, sloping to the mainland.

I watched his feet waken the water

And the ocean break in foam beyond Lobos;

The iron wind struck from the hills.

                  You are tired and corrupt,

You kept the beast under till the fountain's poisoned,

He drips with mange and stinks through the oubliette window.

The promise-breaker war killed whom it freed,

And none living's the cleaner. Yet storm comes, the lions hunt

In the nights striped with lightning. It will come: feed on peace
While the crust holds: to each of you at length a little
Desolation; a pinch of lust or a drop of terror:
Then the lions hunt in the brain of the dying: storm is good,
    storm is good, good creature,
Kind violence, throbbing throat aches with pity.
                         Onorio Vasquez,
Young seer of visions who lives with his six brothers
On the breast of Palo Corona mountain looking northward,
Watches his brother Vidal and Julio the youngest
Play with a hawk they shot from the mountain cloud,
The wing broken. They crucified the creature,
A nail in the broken wing on the barn wall
Between the pink splinters of bone and a nail in the other.
They prod his breast with a wand, no sponge of vinegar,
"Fly down, Jew-beak." The wind streams down the mountain,
The river of cloud streams over: Onorio Vasquez
Never sees anything to the point. What he sees:
The ocean like sleek gray stone perfectly jointed
To the heads and bays, a woman walking upon it,
The curling scud of the storm around her ankles,
Naked and strong, her thighs the height of the mountain,
    walking and weeping,
The shadow of hair under the belly, the jutting breasts like hills,
    the face in the hands and the hair
Streaming north. "Why are you sad, our lady?" "I had only one
    son.
The strange lover never breaks the window-latches again
When Joseph's at synagogue."

Orange eyes, tired and fierce,
They're casting knives at you now, but clumsily, the knives
Quiver in the wood, stern eyes the storm deepens.
Don't wince, topaz eyes.
                    The wind wearies toward evening,
Old Vasquez sends his boys to burn the high pastures
Against the rain: see the autumn fires on the mountain,
        creeping red lakes and crescents
Up the black slope in the slide of the year: that's Vasquez and
        his boys burning the mountain. The high wind
Holds, the low dies, the black curtain flies north.
                            Myrtle Cartwright
Locked the windows but forgot the door, it's a lonely canyon
When the waves flap in the creek-mouth. Andrew's driving
The calves to Monterey, he trusts her, he doesn't know
How all her flesh burned with lascivious desire
Last year, but she remembered her mother and prayed
And God quenched it. Prayer works all right: three times
Rod Stewart came down to see her, he might have been wood
For all she cared. She suffers with constipation,
Tired days and smothering dreams, she's young, life's cheerless,
God sent a little sickness to keep her decent
Since the great prayer. What's that in the west, thunder?
The sea rumbles like thunder but the wind's died down,
Soon it should rain.
                Myrtle Cartwright
Could sleep if her heart would quit moving the bedclothes;
The lighthouse-keeper's daughter little Faith Heriot
Says, "Father the cow's got loose, I must go out
With the storm coming and bring her into the stable.

What would mother do without milk in the morning?"
(Clearly Point Pinos light: stands back from the sea
Among the rolling dunes cupped with old pasture.
Nobody'd keep a cow on the rock at Point Sur.)
This girl never goes near the cowshed but wanders
Into the dunes, the long beam of the light
Swims over and over her head in the high darkness,
The spray of the storm strains through the beam but Faith
Crouches out of the wind in a hollow of the sand
And hears the sea, she rolls on her back in the clear sand
Shuddering, and feels the light lie thwart her hot body
And the sand trickle into the burning places
Comes pale to the house: "Ah, Bossy led me a chase,
Led me a chase." The lighthouse-keeper believes in hell,
His daughter's wild for a lover, his wife sickening toward cancer,
The long yellow beam wheels over the wild sea and the strain
Gathers in the air.
                    Oh crucified
Wings, orange eyes, open?
Always the strain, the straining flesh, who feels what God feels
Knows the straining flesh, the aching desires,
The enormous water straining its bounds, the electric
Strain in the cloud, the strain of the oil in the oil-tanks
At Monterey, aching to burn, the strain of the spinning
Demons that make an atom, straining to fly asunder,
Straining to rest at the center,
The strain in the skull, blind strains, force and counterforce,
Nothing prevails . . .
                    Oh, in storm: storm's kind, kind violence,
When the swollen cloud ached—suddenly

Her charge and agony condensed, slip, the thick dark
Whelps lightning; the air breaks, the twin birth rain falls globed
From the released blackness high up in the air
Ringing like a bell for deliverance.
                                        Many-folded hills
Mouth the black voice that follows the white eye
Opening, universal white eye widening and shut. Myrtle
        Cartwright's
One of those whom thunder shakes with terror: head covered
Against the flashes: "If it should find me and kill me
What's life been worth? Nothing, nothing, nothing, death's
        horrible."
She hears it like a truck driven jolting through heaven
Rumble to the north. "And if I die old:
Nothing, nothing."
                    Vasquez' boys have gone home.
                                        Deep after midnight
        the wind rises, turns iron again,
From east of south, it grinds the heads of the hills, the dunes
        move in the dark at Point Pinos, the sandstone
Lighthouse at Point Sur on the top of the rock is like an
        axhead held against a grindstone.
The high redwoods have quit roaring to scream. Oaks go down
        on the mountain. At Vasquez' place in the yellow
Pallor of dawn the roof of the barn's lifting, his sons cast ropes
        over the timbers. The crucified
Snaps his beak at them. He flies on two nails.
Great eyes, lived all night?
Onorio should have held the rope but it slid through his
        fingers. Onorio Vasquez

Never sees anything to the point. What he sees:
The planted eucalyptuses bent double
All in a row, praying north, "Why everything's praying
And running northward, old hawk anchored with nails
You see that everything goes north like a river.
On a cliff in the north
Stands the strange lover, shines and calls."

In the morning
The inexhaustible clouds flying up from the south
Stream rain, the gullies of the hills grow alive, the creeks flood,
the summer sand-bars
Burst from their mouths, from every sea-mouth wedges of
yellow, yellow tongues. Myrtle Cartwright
Hears the steep cataracts slacken, and then thunder
Pushes the house-walls. "Hear me, God, death's not dreadful.
You heard before when I prayed. Now," she whispers,
"I'll make the bargain," thunder leans on the house-walls, "life's
no value
Like this, I'm going to Stewart's, I can't live empty.
Now Andrew can't come home for every canyon
Vomits its bridge, judgment is yours only,
Death's in your hands." She opens the door on the streaming
Canyon-side, the desperate wind: the dark wet oak-leaves
All in a moment each leaf a distinct fire
Reflects the sharp flash over them: Myrtle Cartwright
Feels the sword plunge: no touch: runs tottering up hill
Through the black voice.

Black pool of oil hidden in the oil-tank
In Monterey felt the sword plunge: touched: the wild heat
Went mad where a little air was, metal curled back,

Fire leaped at the outlet. "Immense ages
We lay under rock, our lust hoarded,
The ache of ignorant desire, the enormous pressure,
The enormous patience, the strain, strain, the strain
Lightened we lay in a steel shell . . . what God kept for us:
Roaring marriage."

                Myrtle Cartwright wins up hill through the
    oak-scrub
And through the rain, the wind at the summit
Knocks her breasts and her mouth, she crouches in the mud,
Feels herself four-foot like a beast and the lightning
Will come from behind and cover her, the wolf of white fire,
Force the cold flesh, cling with his forepaws. "Oh, death's
What I was after." She runs on the road northward, the wind
    behind her,
The lightnings like white doves hovering her head, harmless as
    pigeons, through great bars of black noise.
She lifts her wet arms. "Come, doves."

                    The oil-tank boils with joy in
    the north, one among ten, one tank
Burns, the nine others wait, feel warmth, dim change of
    patience. This one roars with fulfilled desire,
The ring-bound molecules splitting, the atoms dancing apart,
    marrying the air.
              Myrtle Cartwright
Knocks on her door: "Oh, I've come. Here's what you wanted."
    (In the yellow inland no rain but the same lightning,
And it lights a forest.) He leads her into the barn because there
    are people in the house.

In the north the oil-tanks
Catch from the first, the ring-bound molecules splitting, the
    atoms dancing apart, marrying the air.
The marriage-bound thighs opening, on the stiff white straw,
    the nerves of fire, the ganglia like stars.

Don't you see any vision Onorio Vasquez? "No, for the topazes
Have dulled out of his head, he soars on two nails,
Dead hawk over the coast. Oh little brother
Julio, if you could drive nails through my hands
I'd stand against the door: through the middle of the palms:
And take the hawk's place, you could throw knives at me.
I'd give you my saddle and the big bridle, Julio,
With the bit that rings and rings when the horse twirls it."
He smiles. "You'd see the lights flicker in my hair."
He smiles craftily. "You'd live long and be rich,
And nobody could beat you in running or riding."
He chatters his teeth. "It is necessary for someone to be
    fastened with nails.
And Jew-beak died in the night. Jew-beak is dead."

FROM

CAWDOR

THE OLD MAN'S DREAM
AFTER HE DIED

FROM *CAWDOR*

Gently with delicate mindless fingers
Decomposition began to pick and caress the unstable chemistry
Of the cells of the brain; Oh very gently, as the first weak breath of
   wind in a wood: the storm is still far,
The leaves are stirred faintly to a gentle whispering: the nerve-cells,
   by what would soon destroy them, were stirred
To a gentle whispering. Or one might say the brain began to glow,
   with its own light, in the starless
Darkness under the dead bone sky; like bits of rotting wood on the
   floor of the night forest
Warm rains have soaked, you see them beside the path shine like
   vague eyes. So gently the dead man's brain
Glowing by itself made and enjoyed its dream.

           The nights of many
  years before this time
He had been dreaming the sweetness of death, as a starved man
   dreams bread, but now decomposition
Reversed the chemistry; who had adored in sleep under so many
   disguises the dark redeemer
In death across a thousand metaphors of form and action celebrated
   life. Whatever he had wanted
To do or become was now accomplished, each bud that had been
   nipped and fallen grew out to a branch,
Sparks of desire forty years quenched flamed up fulfilment.

Out of time, undistracted by the nudging pulse-beat, perfectly
    real to itself being insulated
From all touch of reality the dream triumphed, building from
    past experience present paradise
More intense as the decay quickened, but ever more primitive as
    it proceeded, until the ecstasy
Soared through a flighty carnival of wines and women to the
    simple delight of eating flesh, and tended
Even higher, to an unconditional delight. But then the
    interconnections between the groups of the brain
Failing, the dreamer and the dream split into multitude. Soon
    the altered cells became unfit to express
Any human or at all describable form of consciousness.

                                                    Pain and

        pleasure are not to be thought
Important enough to require balancing: these flashes of
    post-mortal felicity by mindless decay
Played on the breaking harp by no means countervalued the
    excess of previous pain. Such discords
In the passionate terms of human experience are not resolved,
    nor worth it.

THE CAGED EAGLE'S
DEATH DREAM

FROM *CAWDOR*

While George went to the house
For his revolver, Michal climbed up the hill
Weeping; but when he came with death in his hand
She'd not go away, but watched. At the one shot
The great dark bird leaped at the roof of the cage
In silence and struck the wood; it fell, then suddenly
Looked small and soft, muffled in its folded wings.

The nerves of men after they die dream dimly
And dwindle into their peace; they are not very passionate,
And what they had was mostly spent while they lived.
They are sieves for leaking desire; they have many pleasures
And conversations; their dreams too are like that.
The unsocial birds are a greater race;
Cold-eyed, and their blood burns. What leaped up to death,
The extension of one storm-dark wing filling its world,
Was more than the soft garment that fell. Something had flown
        away. Oh cage-hoarded desire,
Like the blade of a breaking wave reaped by the wind, or flame
        rising from fire, or cloud-coiled lightning
Suddenly unfurled in the cave of heaven: I that am stationed, and
        cold at heart, incapable of burning,
My blood like standing sea-water lapped in a stone pool, my desire
        to the rock, how can I speak of you?
Mine will go down to the deep rock.

This rose,
Possessing the air over its emptied prison,
The eager powers at its shoulders waving shadowless
Unwound the ever-widened spirals of flight
As a star light, it spins the night-stabbing threads
From its own strength and substance: so the aquiline desire
Burned itself into meteor freedom and spired
Higher still, and saw the mountain-dividing
Canyon of its captivity (that was to Cawdor
Almost his world) like an old crack in a wall,
Violet-shadowed and gold-lighted; the little stain
Spilt on the floor of the crack was the strong forest;
The grain of sand was the Rock. A speck, an atomic
Center of power clouded in its own smoke
Ran and cried in the crack; it was Cawdor; the other
Points of humanity had neither weight nor shining
To prick the eyes of even an eagle's passion.

This burned and soared. The shining ocean below lay on the
    shore
Like the great shield of the moon come down, rolling bright rim
    to rim with the earth. Against it the multiform
And many-canyoned coast-range hills were gathered into one
    carven mountain, one modulated
Eagle's cry made stone, stopping the strength of the sea. The
    beaked and winged effluence
Felt the air foam under its throat and saw
The mountain sun-cup Tassajara, where fawns
Dance in the steam of the hot fountains at dawn,
Smoothed out, and the high strained ridges beyond Cachagua,

Where the rivers are born and the last condor is dead,
Flatten, and a hundred miles toward morning the Sierras
Dawn with their peaks of snow, and dwindle and smooth down
On the globed earth.

It saw from the height and desert space of
    unbreathable air
Where meteors make green fire and die, the ocean dropping
    westward to the girdle of the pearls of dawn
And the hinder edge of the night sliding toward Asia; it saw far
    under eastward the April-delighted
Continent; and time relaxing about it now, abstracted from
    being, it saw the eagles destroyed,
Mean generations of gulls and crows taking their world: turn for
    turn in the air, as on earth
The white faces drove out the brown. It saw the white decayed
    and the brown from Asia returning;
It saw men learn to outfly the hawk's brood and forget it again;
    it saw men cover the earth and again
Devour each other and hide in caverns, be scarce as wolves. It
    neither wondered nor cared, and it saw
Growth and decay alternate forever, and the tides returning.

It saw, according to the sight of its kind, the archetype
Body of life a beaked carnivorous desire
Self-upheld on storm-broad wings: but the eyes
Were spouts of blood; the eyes were gashed out; dark blood
Ran from the ruinous eye-pits to the hook of the beak
And rained on the waste spaces of empty heaven.

Yet the great Life continued; yet the great Life
Was beautiful, and she drank her defeat, and devoured
Her famine for food.

                  There the eagle's phantom perceived
Its prison and its wound were not its peculiar wretchedness,
All that lives was maimed and bleeding, caged or in blindness,
Lopped at the ends with death and conception, and shrewd
Cautery of pain on the stumps to stifle the blood, but not
Refrains for all that; life was more than its functions
And accidents, more important than its pains and pleasures,
A torch to burn in with pride, a necessary
Ecstasy in the run of the cold substance,
And scape-goat of the greater world. (But as for me,
I have heard the summer dust crying to be born
As much as ever flesh cried to be quiet.)
Pouring itself on fulfilment the eagle's passion
Left life behind and flew at the sun, its father.
The great unreal talons took peace for prey
Exultantly, their death beyond death; stooped upward, and
      struck
Peace like a white fawn in a dell of fire.

BIXBY'S LANDING

They burned lime on the hill and dropped it down here in an
    iron car
On a long cable; here the ships warped in
And took their loads from the engine, the water is deep to the
    cliff. The car
Hangs halfway over in the gape of the gorge,
Stationed like a north star above the peaks of the redwoods,
    iron perch
For the little red hawks when they cease from hovering
When they've struck prey; the spider's fling of a cable rust-glued
    to the pulleys.
The laborers are gone, but what a good multitude
Is here in return: the rich-lichened rock, the rose-tipped
    stone-crop, the constant
Ocean's voices, the cloud-lighted space.
The kilns are cold on the hill but here in the rust of the broken
    boiler
Quick lizards lighten, and a rattlesnake flows
Down the cracked masonry, over the crumbled fire-brick. In the
    rotting timbers
And roofless platforms all the free companies
Of windy grasses have root and make seed; wild buckwheat
    blooms in the fat
Weather-slacked lime from the bursted barrels.
Two duckhawks darting in the sky of their cliff-hung nest are
    the voice of the headland.

Wine-hearted solitude, our mother the wilderness,
Men's failures are often as beautiful as men's triumphs, but your
    returnings
Are even more precious than your first presence.

FAWN'S FOSTER MOTHER

The old woman sits on a bench before the door and quarrels
With her meager pale demoralized daughter.
Once when I passed I found her alone, laughing in the sun
And saying that when she was first married
She lived in the old farmhouse up Garapatas Canyon.
(It is empty now, the roof has fallen
But the log walls hang on the stone foundation; the redwoods
Have all been cut down, the oaks are standing;
The place is now more solitary than ever before.)
"When I was nursing my second baby
My husband found a day-old fawn hid in a fern-brake
And brought it; I put its mouth to the breast
Rather than let it starve, I had milk enough for three babies.
Hey, how it sucked, the little nuzzler,
Digging its little hoofs like quills into my stomach.
I had more joy from that than from the others."
Her face is deformed with age, furrowed like a bad road
With market-wagons, mean cares and decay.
She is thrown up to the surface of things, a cell of dry skin
Soon to be shed from the earth's old eyebrows,
I see that once in her spring she lived in the streaming arteries,
The stir of the world, the music of the mountain.

A REDEEMER

The road had steepened and the sun sharpened on the high
    ridges; the stream probably was dry,
Certainly not to be come to down the pit of the canyon. We
    stopped for water at the one farm
In all that mountain. The trough was cracked with drought, the
    moss on the boards dead, but an old dog
Rose like a wooden toy at the house-door silently. I said "There
    will be water somewhere about,"
And when I knocked a man showed us a spring of water.
    Though his hair was nearly white I judged him
Forty years old at most. His eyes and voice were muted. It is
    likely he kept his hands hidden,
I failed to see them until we had dipped the spring. He stood
    then on the lip of the great slope
And looked westward over an incredible country to the far hills
    that dammed the sea-fog: it billowed
Above them, cascaded over them, it never crossed them, gray
    standing flood. He stood gazing, his hands
Were clasped behind him; I caught a glimpse of serous red
    under the fingers, and looking sharply
When they drew apart saw that both hands were wounded.
    I said "Your hands are hurt." He twitched them from
    sight,
But after a moment having earnestly eyed me displayed them.
    The wounds were in the hearts of the palms,
Pierced to the backs like stigmata of crucifixion. The horrible
    raw flesh protruded, glistening

And granular, not scabbed, nor a sign of infection. "These are
old wounds." He answered, "Yes. They don't heal." He
stood

Moving his lips in silence, his back against that fabulous basin
of mountains, fold beyond fold,

Patches of forest and scarps of rock, high domes of dead gray
pasture and gray beds of dry rivers,

Clear and particular in the burning air, too bright to appear
real, to the last range

The fog from the ocean like a stretched compacted
thunderstorm overhung; and he said gravely:

"I pick them open. I made them long ago with a clean steel. It
is only a little to pay—"

He stretched and flexed the fingers, I saw his sunburnt lips
whiten in a line, compressed together,

"If only it proves enough for a time—to save so many." I
searched his face for madness but that

Is often invisible, a subtle spirit. "There never," he said, "was
any people earned so much ruin.

I love them, I am trying to suffer for them. It would be bad if I
should die, I am careful

Against excess." "You think of the wounds," I said, "of Jesus?"
He laughed angrily and frowned, stroking

The fingers of one hand with the other. "Religion is the
people's opium. Your little Jew-God?

My pain," he said with pride, "is voluntary.

They have done what never was done before. Not as a people
takes a land to love it and be fed,

A little, according to need and love, and again a little; sparing
the country tribes, mixing

Their blood with theirs, their minds with all the rocks and
	rivers, their flesh with the soil: no, without hunger
Wasting the world and your own labor, without love possessing,
	not even your hands to the dirt but plows
Like blades of knives; heartless machines; houses of steel: using
	and despising the patient earth . . .
Oh, as a rich man eats a forest for profit and a field for vanity,
	so you came west and raped
The continent and brushed its people to death. Without need,
	the weak skirmishing hunters, and without mercy.
Well, God's a scarecrow; no vengeance out of old rags. But
	there are acts breeding their own reversals
In their own bellies from the first day. I am here" he said—and
	broke off suddenly and said "They take horses
And give them sicknesses through hollow needles, their blood
	saves babies: I am here on the mountain making
Antitoxin for all the happy towns and farms, the lovely
	blameless children, the terrible
Arrogant cities. I used to think them terrible: their gray
	prosperity, their pride: from up here
Specks of mildew.

			But when I am dead and all you with whole
	hands think of nothing but happiness,
Will you go mad and kill each other? Or horror come over the
	ocean on wings and cover your sun?
I wish," he said trembling, "I had never been born."

His wife came from the door while he was talking. Mine asked
	her quietly, "Do you live all alone here,

Are you not afraid?" "Certainly not," she answered, "he is
   always gentle and loving. I have no complaint
Except his groans in the night keep me awake often. But when I
   think of other women's
Troubles: my own daughter's: I'm older than my husband, I
   have been married before: deep is my peace."

If you should look for this place after a handful of lifetimes:
Perhaps of my planted forest a few
May stand yet, dark-leaved Australians or the coast cypress,
    haggard
With storm-drift; but fire and the axe are devils.
Look for foundations of sea-worn granite, my fingers had the art
To make stone love stone, you will find some remnant.
But if you should look in your idleness after ten thousand years:
It is the granite knoll on the granite
And lava tongue in the midst of the bay, by the mouth of the
    Carmel
River-valley, these four will remain
In the change of names. You will know it by the wild
    sea-fragrance of wind
Though the ocean may have climbed or retired a little;
You will know it by the valley inland that our sun and our
    moon were born from
Before the poles changed; and Orion in December
Evenings was strung in the throat of the valley like a
    lamp-lighted bridge.
Come in the morning you will see white gulls
Weaving a dance over blue water, the wane of the moon
Their dance-companion, a ghost walking
By daylight, but wider and whiter than any bird in the world.
My ghost you needn't look for; it is probably
Here, but a dark one, deep in the granite, not dancing on wind
With the mad wings and the day moon.

HURT HAWKS

I

The broken pillar of the wing jags from the clotted shoulder,
The wing trails like a banner in defeat,

   No more to use the sky forever but live with famine
And pain a few days: cat nor coyote
Will shorten the week of waiting for death, there is game
     without talons.

He stands under the oak-bush and waits
The lame feet of salvation; at night he remembers freedom
And flies in a dream, the dawns ruin it.

He is strong and pain is worse to the strong, incapacity is
     worse.

The curs of the day come and torment him
At distance, no one but death the redeemer will humble that
     head,

The intrepid readiness, the terrible eyes.
The wild God of the world is sometimes merciful to those
That ask mercy, not often to the arrogant.

You do not know him, you communal people, or you have
     forgotten him;

Intemperate and savage, the hawk remembers him;
Beautiful and wild, the hawks, and men that are dying,
     remember him.

II

I'd sooner, except the penalties, kill a man than a hawk;
     but the great redtail

Had nothing left but unable misery

From the bone too shattered for mending, the wing that trailed
    under his talons when he moved.
We had fed him six weeks, I gave him freedom,
He wandered over the foreland hill and returned in the evening,
    asking for death,
Not like a beggar, still eyed with the old
Implacable arrogance. I gave him the lead gift in the twilight.
    What fell was relaxed,
Owl-downy, soft feminine feathers; but what
Soared: the fierce rush: the night-herons by the flooded river
    cried fear at its rising
Before it was quite unsheathed from reality.

MEDITATION ON SAVIORS

I

When I considered it too closely, when I wore it like an element
    and smelt it like water,
Life is become less lovely, the net nearer than the skin, a little
    troublesome, a little terrible.

I pledged myself awhile ago not to seek refuge, neither in death nor
    in a walled garden,
In lies nor gated loyalties, nor in the gates of contempt, that
    easily lock the world out of doors.

Here on the rock it is great and beautiful, here on the foam-wet
    granite sea-fang it is easy to praise
Life and water and the shining stones: but whose cattle are the
    herds of the people that one should love them?

If they were yours, then you might take a cattle-breeder's delight in
    the herds of the future. Not yours.
Where the power ends let love, before it sours to jealousy. Leave
    the joys of government to Caesar.

Who is born when the world wanes, when the brave soul of the
    world falls on decay in the flesh increasing
Comes one with a great level mind, sufficient vision, sufficient
    blindness, and clemency for love.

This is the breath of rottenness I smelt; from the world waiting,
    stalled between storms, decaying a little,
Bitterly afraid to be hurt, but knowing it cannot draw the savior
    Caesar but out of the blood-bath.

The apes of Christ lift up their hands to praise love: but
    wisdom without love is the present savior,
Power without hatred, mind like a many-bladed machine
    subduing the world with deep indifference.

The apes of Christ itch for a sickness they have never known;
    words and the little envies will hardly
Measure against that blinding fire behind the tragic eyes they
    have never dared to confront.

11

Point Lobos lies over the hollowed water like a humped whale
    swimming to shoal; Point Lobos
Was wounded with that fire; the hills at Point Sur endured it;
    the palace at Thebes; the hill Calvary.

Out of incestuous love power and then ruin. A man forcing the
    imaginations of men,
Possessing with love and power the people: a man defiling his
    own household with impious desire.

King Oedipus reeling blinded from the palace doorway, red
    tears pouring from the torn pits
Under the forehead; and the young Jew writhing on the domed
    hill in the earthquake, against the eclipse

Frightfully uplifted for having turned inward to love the people:—
    that root was so sweet Oh, dreadful agonist?—
I saw the same pierced feet, that walked in the same crime to its
    expiation; I heard the same cry.

A bad mountain to build your world on. Am I another keeper
    of the people, that on my own shore,
On the gray rock, by the grooved mass of the ocean, the
    sicknesses I left behind me concern me?

Here where the surf has come incredible ways out of the
    splendid west, over the deeps
Light nor life sounds forever; here where enormous sundowns
    flower and burn through color to quietness;

Then the ecstasy of the stars is present? As for the people, I
    have found my rock, let them find theirs.
Let them lie down at Caesar's feet and be saved; and he in his
    time reap their daggers of gratitude.

III
Yet I am the one made pledges against the refuge contempt,
    that easily locks the world out of doors.
This people as much as the sea-granite is part of the God from
    whom I desire not to be fugitive.

I see them: they are always crying. The shored Pacific makes
    perpetual music, and the stone mountains
Their music of silence, the stars blow long pipings of light: the
    people are always crying in their hearts.

One need not pity; certainly one must not love. But who has seen
  peace, if he should tell them where peace
Lives in the world . . . they would be powerless to understand;
  and he is not willing to be reinvolved.

IV

How should one caught in the stone of his own person dare tell
  the people anything but relative to that?
But if a man could hold in his mind all the conditions at once,
  of man and woman, of civilized

And barbarous, of sick and well, of happy and under torture, of
  living and dead, of human and not
Human, and dimly all the human future:—what should persuade
  him to speak? And what could his words change?

The mountain ahead of the world is not forming but fixed. But
  the man's words would be fixed also,
Part of that mountain, under equal compulsion; under the same
  present compulsion in the iron consistency.

And nobody sees good or evil but out of a brain a hundred
  centuries quieted, some desert
Prophet's, a man humped like a camel, gone mad between the
  mud-walled village and the mountain sepulchres.

V

Broad wagons before sunrise bring food into the city from the
  open farms, and the people are fed.
They import and they consume reality. Before sunrise a hawk in
  the desert made them their thoughts.

Here is an anxious people, rank with suppressed blood-thirstiness.
    Among the mild and unwarlike
Gautama needed but live greatly and be heard, Confucius
    needed but live greatly and be heard.

This people has not outgrown blood-sacrifice, one must writhe
    on the high cross to catch at their memories;
The price is known. I have quieted love; for love of the people I
    would not do it. For power I would do it.

—But that stands against reason: what is power to a dead man,
    dead under torture?—What is power to a man
Living, after the flesh is content? Reason is never a root, neither
    of act nor desire.

For power living I would never do it; they are not delightful to
    touch, one wants to be separate. For power
After the nerves are put away underground, to lighten the
    abstract unborn children toward peace . . .

A man might have paid anguish indeed. Except he had found
    the standing sea-rock that even this last
Temptation breaks on; quieter than death but lovelier; peace
    that quiets the desire even of praising it.

VII

Yet look: are they not pitiable? No: if they lived forever they
    would be pitiable:
But a huge gift reserved quite overwhelms them at the end; they
    are able then to be still and not cry.

And having touched a little of the beauty and seen a little of the
    beauty of things, magically grow
Across the funeral fire or the hidden stench of burial themselves
    into the beauty they admired,

Themselves into the God, themselves into the sacred steep
    unconsciousness they used to mimic
Asleep between lamp's death and dawn, while the last drunkard
    stumbled homeward down the dark street.

They are not to be pitied but very fortunate; they need no
    savior, salvation comes and takes them by force,
It gathers them into the great kingdoms of dust and stone, the
    blown storms, the stream's-end ocean.

With this advantage over their granite grave-marks, of having
    realized the petulant human consciousness
Before, and then the greatness, the peace: drunk from both
    pitchers: these to be pitied? These not fortunate?

But while he lives let each man make his health in his mind, to
    love the coast opposite humanity
And so be freed of love, laying it like bread on the waters; it is
    worst turned inward, it is best shot farthest.

Love, the mad wine of good and evil, the saint's and
    murderer's, the mote in the eye that makes its object
Shine the sun black; the trap in which it is better to catch the
    inhuman God than the hunter's own image.

FROM
DEAR JUDAS

THE BROKEN BALANCE

The people buying and selling, consuming pleasures, talking
   in the archways,
Were all suddenly struck quiet
And ran from under stone to look up at the sky: so shrill and
   mournful,
So fierce and final, a brazen
Pealing of trumpets high up in the air, in the summer blue over
   Tuscany.
They marveled; the soothsayers answered:
"Although the Gods are little troubled toward men, at the end
   of each period
A sign is declared in heaven
Indicating new times, new customs, a changed people; the
   Romans
Rule, and Etruria is finished;
A wise mariner will trim the sails to the wind."

                    I heard yesterday
So shrill and mournful a trumpet-blast,
It was hard to be wise. . . . You must eat change and endure;
   not be much troubled
For the people; they will have their happiness.
When the republic grows too heavy to endure, then Cæsar will
   carry it;
When life grows hateful, there's power . . .

II. TO THE CHILDREN

Power's good; life is not always good but power's good.

So you must think when abundance

Makes pawns of people and all the loaves are one dough.

The steep singleness of passion

Dies; they will say, "What was that?" but the power triumphs.

Loveliness will live under glass

And beauty will go savage in the secret mountains.

There is beauty in power also.

You children must widen your minds' eyes to take mountains

Instead of faces, and millions

Instead of persons; not to hate life; and massed power

After the lone hawk's dead.

III

That light blood-loving weasel, a tongue of yellow

Fire licking the sides of the gray stones,

Has a more passionate and more pure heart

In the snake-slender flanks than man can imagine;

But he is betrayed by his own courage,

The man who kills him is like a cloud hiding a star.

Then praise the jewel-eyed hawk and the tall blue heron;

The black cormorants that fatten their sea-rock

With shining slime; even that ruiner of anthills

The red-shafted woodpecker flying,

A white star between blood-color wing-clouds,

Across the glades of the wood and the green lakes of shade.

These live their felt natures; they know their norm

And live it to the brim; they understand life.

While men moulding themselves to the anthill have choked
Their natures until the souls die in them;
They have sold themselves for toys and protection:
No, but consider awhile: what else? Men sold for toys.

Uneasy and fractional people, having no center
But in the eyes and mouths that surround them,
Having no function but to serve and support
Civilization, the enemy of man,
No wonder they live insanely, and desire
With their tongues, progress; with their eyes, pleasure; with
        their hearts, death.

Their ancestors were good hunters, good herdsmen and
        swordsmen,
But now the world is turned upside down;
The good do evil, the hope's in criminals; in vice
That dissolves the cities and war to destroy them.
Through wars and corruptions the house will fall.
Mourn whom it falls on. Be glad: the house is mined, it will fall.
IV
Rain, hail and brutal sun, the plow in the roots,
The pitiless pruning-iron in the branches,
Strengthen the vines, they are all feeding friends
Or powerless foes until the grapes purple.
But when you have ripened your berries it is time to begin to
        perish.

The world sickens with change, rain becomes poison,
The earth is a pit, it is time to perish.

The vines are fey, the very kindness of nature
Corrupts what her cruelty before strengthened.
When you stand on the peak of time it is time to begin to
   perish.

Reach down the long morbid roots that forget the plow,
Discover the depths; let the long pale tendrils
Spend all to discover the sky, now nothing is good
But only the steel mirrors of discovery . . .
And the beautiful enormous dawns of time, after we perish.
v
Mourning the broken balance, the hopeless prostration of the
   earth
Under men's hands and their minds,
The beautiful places killed like rabbits to make a city,
The spreading fungus, the slime-threads
And spores; my own coast's obscene future: I remember the
   farther
Future, and the last man dying
Without succession under the confident eyes of the stars.
It was only a moment's accident,
The race that plagued us; the world resumes the old lonely
   immortal
Splendor; from here I can even
Perceive that that snuffed candle had something . . . a fantastic
   virtue,
A faint and unshapely pathos . . .
So death will flatter them at last: what, even the bald ape's
   by-shot
Was moderately admirable?

VI. PALINODE

All summer neither rain nor wave washes the cormorants'
Perch, and their droppings have painted it shining white.
If the excrement of fish-eaters makes the brown rock a
    snow-mountain
At noon, a rose in the morning, a beacon at moonrise
On the black water: it is barely possible that even men's present
Lives are something; their arts and sciences (by moonlight)
Not wholly ridiculous, nor their cities merely an offense.

VII

Under my windows, between the road and the sea-cliff, bitter
    wild grass
Stands narrowed between the people and the storm.
The ocean winter after winter gnaws at its earth, the wheels and
    the feet
Summer after summer encroach and destroy.
Stubborn green life, for the cliff-eater I cannot comfort you,
    ignorant which color,
Gray-blue or pale-green, will please the late stars;
But laugh at the other, your seed shall enjoy wonderful
    vengeances and suck
The arteries and walk in triumph on the faces.

EVENING EBB

The ocean has not been so quiet for a long while; five
    night-herons
Fly shorelong voiceless in the hush of the air
Over the calm of an ebb that almost mirrors their wings.
The sun has gone down, and the water has gone down
From the weed-clad rock, but the distant cloud-wall rises. The
    ebb whispers.
Great cloud-shadows float in the opal water.
Through rifts in the screen of the world pale gold gleams, and
    the evening
Star suddenly glides like a flying torch.
As if we had not been meant to see her; rehearsing behind
The screen of the world for another audience.

# HANDS

Inside a cave in a narrow canyon near Tassajara
The vault of rock is painted with hands,
A multitude of hands in the twilight, a cloud of men's palms,
   no more,
No other picture. There's no one to say
Whether the brown shy quiet people who are dead intended
Religion or magic, or made their tracings
In the idleness of art; but over the division of years these
   careful
Signs-manual are now like a sealed message
Saying: "Look: we also were human; we had hands, not paws.
   All hail
You people with the cleverer hands, our supplanters
In the beautiful country; enjoy her a season, her beauty, and
   come down
And be supplanted; for you also are human."

At night, toward dawn, all the lights of the shore have died,
And the wind moves. Moves in the dark
The sleeping power of the ocean, no more beastlike than
    manlike,
Not to be compared; itself and itself.
Its breath blown shoreward huddles the world with a fog; no
    stars
Dance in heaven; no ship's light glances.
I see the heavy granite bodies of the rocks of the headland,
That were ancient here before Egypt had pyramids,
Bulk on the gray of the sky, and beyond them the jets of young
    trees
I planted the year of the Versailles peace.
But here is the final unridiculous peace. Before the first man
Here were the stones, the ocean, the cypresses,
And the pallid region in the stone-rough dome of fog where the
    moon
Falls on the west. Here is reality.
The other is a spectral episode: after the inquisitive animal's
Amusements are quiet: the dark glory.

THE HUMANIST'S TRAGEDY

Not like a beast borne on the flood of passion, boat without
    oars, but mindful of all his dignity
As human being, a king and a Greek, King Pentheus: "Tell him
    that we will reverence the Gods we have,
But not minded to increase the burden. What new ones ship
    raging like beasts from Asia by the islands
We've whips for, here in Thebes. Tell him to take his
    magic-drunken women and be off." The messenger
Went up to the mountain wood; needles of pine stuck in the
    sandal-straps of the man returning
At noon and saying: "He could not hear me, O King. I shouted
    aloud, clothed in the king's authority,
Showing him the wand I carried: the God's . . . I say the
    stranger's . . . eyes like blue ice looked through my body
As if I had been an open window in the breast of a wall.
    He bored through me toward Thebes and answered
Not me, the raging laughing women: 'They have Isemenus to
    drink of, and Dirce, and all the fountains,
Must they have wine too?' What more he said, my lord, I
    cannot remember. But I, having seen more
Than I dare tell, turned home." "Ten spearmen," the king
    answered, biting the bearded lip, "will do it.
What more saw you? Dread not to tell, obscene or magic. We
    are master of ourself as of this people.
Not like a beast borne on the flood of passion, boat without
    oars, but mindful of all our dignity
As human being, a king and a Greek: no random lightning of
    anger will stab the messenger. We're sane still

Though the air swarms." The messenger: "My lord, my
        lord . . ." And the king: "Out with it." "The lady Agave,
        my lord."
"Our mother," the king answered frowning. "—Was in the
        mountain with the other women, dancing, adoring."
King Pentheus' knuckles, of the hand that held the long
Smooth-shaven staff tipped with the head of a man carved in
        pale ivory, whitened, and the hand reddened
Under the scant stipple of black hair. More than that was no
        motion. "Well, she was in the mountain,"
He answered, "My mother was there," the king housing his
        wrath in hard self-mastery. He had the chariot
Horsed, and rode swiftly toward Cythaeron; the glens and the
        slope bristled with forest. In a glade he found them.
He had come alone; the charioteer stayed by the sweating
        horses. Without awe, without pleasure,
As a man spies on noxious beasts, he standing hidden spied on
        the rabid choir of the God.
They had pine-cone-tipped wands, they went half naked, they
        were hoarse with insane song; foam from their mouths,
        mingled
With wine and sweat, ran down their bodies. O fools, boats
        without oars borne on the flood of passion,
Forgetting utterly all the dignity of man, the pride of the only
        self-commanding animal,
That captains his own soul and controls even
Fate, for a space. The only animal that turns means to an end.
        "What end? Oh, but what end?"
It cried under his mind, "Increase the city? subdue the earth?

Breed slaves and cattle, and one's own
Off-shots, fed and secure? Ah fruitful-fruitless
Generations forever and ever. . . . For pleasure"—he spat on
   the earth—"the slight collectible pleasure
Surplus to pain?" Then recollecting all his dignity as human
   being, a king and a Greek,
He heard with hostile ears the hoarse and beastlike choir of the
   worshipers: "O sisters, we have found an opening,
We have hewn in the stone and mortar
A wild strait gateway,
Slit eyes in the mask, sisters,
Entered the mountain.
We shall be sad to-morrow when the wine dies,
The God dies from our blood;
To-day in the forest
We are fire and have found an opening."
His own mother Agave singing. Endure a little. If one could
   understand their fountain
Of madness. Her shame to-morrow: not punishment enough:
   prison in the house. "O sisters, we have found an
   opening":
What opening?

   The boys from Thebes to be whipped, the
Theban women shut up a fortnight, the God and his
   Thracian
Satyrs and women . . . "The generations," he thought suddenly,
   "aspire. They better; they climb; as I
Am better than this weak suggestible woman my mother. Had I
   forgotten a moment the end

Of being? To increase the power, collectedness and dignity of
　　man.—A more collected and dignified
Creature," he groaned, "to die and stink."

　　　　　　　　　　　　　　That moment like a tall ship
　　breasting through water the God
Passed, the high head, the shining hair and the blond shoulders,
　　trailing a wake of ecstasy like foam
Across the multitude of faces like waves, his frantic worshipers.
　　He anchored among them smiling
In the wild midst, and said softly: "When you are dead you
　　become part of peace; let no man
Dream more of death; there is neither sight nor hearing nor any
　　wonder; none of us Gods enters it.
You become part of peace, part of the sacred beauty, but *having*
　　no part: as if a flute-player
Should make beauty but hear none, being deaf and senseless.
　　But living if you will
It is possible for you to break prison of yourselves and enter the
　　nature of things and use the beauty.
Wine and lawlessness, art and music, love, self-torture, religion,
Are means but are not needful, contemplation will do it. Only
　　to break human collectedness.
The least shepherd on Cythaeron, if he dares, might do it.
　　But you being neophyte all, Thracians and Thebans,
Are indeed somewhat wild, somewhat too drunken."

　　　　　　　　　　　　　King Pentheus then, seeing his
　　enemy, but ever
Stately mindful of all his dignity, as human being, a king and a
　　Greek, entered among them

Angrily to fetch his mother. Agave cried out,
"Sisters: a lion stalking us, a wild beast of the pinewood, or is it
    a wolf?" She leading eagerly,
Full of the courage that the God had taught them, rushed on
    her son not known, and the others raging
Joined her; the frantic voices, the tearing fingers, the teeth and
    the madness . . .

                    The God and his people went down
Toward Thebes, Agave dancing before them, the head of her
    son the triumph in her hands, the beard and the blood:
"A lion I have killed in the mountain,
Thebans, the head of a lion my own hands hunted,
With my hands, a lion!"

FROM

DESCENT TO
THE DEAD

SHANE O'NEILL'S CAIRN

TO U.J.

When you and I on the Palos Verdes cliff
Found life more desperate than dear,
And when we hawked at it on the lake by Seattle,
In the west of the world, where hardly
Anything has died yet: we'd not have been sorry, Una,
But surprised, to foresee this gray
Coast in our days, the gray waters of the Moyle
Below us, and under our feet
The heavy black stones of the cairn of the lord of Ulster.
A man of blood who died bloodily
Four centuries ago: but death's nothing, and life,
From a high death-mark on a headland
Of this dim island of burials, is nothing either.
How beautiful are both these nothings.

OSSIAN'S GRAVE

PREHISTORIC MONUMENT NEAR
CUSHENDALL IN ANTRIM

Steep up in Lubitavish townland stands
A ring of great stones like fangs, the shafts of the stones
Grown up with thousands of years of gradual turf,
The fangs of the stones still biting skyward; and hard
Against the stone ring, the oblong enclosure
Of an old grave guarded with erect slabs; gray rocks
Backed by broken thorn-trees, over the gorge of Glenaan;
It is called Ossian's Grave. Ossian rests high then,
Haughtily alone.
If there were any fame or burial or monument
For me to envy,
Warrior and poet they should be yours and yours.

For this is the pure fame, not caged in a poem,
Fabulous, a glory untroubled with works, a name in the north
Like a mountain in the mist, like Aura
Heavy with heather and the dark gray rocks, or Trostan
Dark purple in the cloud: happier than what the wings
And imperfections of work hover like vultures
Above the carcass.

                    I also make a remembered name;
And I shall return home to the granite stones
On my cliff over the greatest ocean
To be blind ashes under the butts of the stones:

As you here under the fanged limestone columns
Are said to lie, over the narrow north straits
Toward Scotland, and the quick-tempered Moyle. But written
    reminders
Will blot for too long a year the bare sunlight
Above my rock lair, heavy black birds
Over the field and the blood of the lost battle.

Oh but we lived splendidly
In the brief light of day
Who now twist in our graves.
You in the guard of the fanged
Erect stones; and the man-slayer
Shane O'Neill dreams yonder at Cushendun
Crushed under his cairn;
And Hugh McQuillan under his cairn
By his lost field in the bog on Aura;
And I a foreigner, one who has come to the country of the
    dead
Before I was called,
To eat the bitter dust of my ancestors;
And thousands on tens of thousands in the thronged earth
Under the rotting freestone tablets
At the bases of broken round towers;
And the great Connaught queen on her mountain-summit
The high cloud hoods, it creeps through the eyes of the cairn.

We dead have our peculiar pleasures, of not
Doing, of not feeling, of not being.
Enough has been felt, enough done, Oh and surely

Enough of humanity has been. We lie under stones
Or drift through the endless northern twilights
And draw over our pale survivors the net of our dream.
All their lives are less
Substantial than one of our deaths, and they cut turf
Or stoop in the steep
Short furrows, or drive the red carts, like weeds waving
Under the glass of water in a locked bay,
Which neither the wind nor the wave nor their own will
Moves; when they seem to awake
It is only to madden in their dog-days for memories of dreams
That lost all meaning many centuries ago.

Oh but we lived splendidly
In the brief light of day,
You with hounds on the mountain
And princes in palaces,
I on the western cliff
In the rages of the sun:
Now you lie grandly under your stones
But I in a peasant's hut
Eat bread bitter with the dust of dead men;
The water I draw at the spring has been shed for tears
Ten thousand times,
Or wander through the endless northern twilights
From the rath to the cairn, through fields
Where every field-stone's been handled
Ten thousand times,
In a uterine country, soft
And wet and worn out, like an old womb
That I have returned to, being dead.

Oh but we lived splendidly
Who now twist in our graves.
The mountains are alive;
Tievebuilleagh lives, Trostan lives,
Lurigethan lives;
And Aura, the black-faced sheep in the belled heather;
And the swan-haunted loughs; but also a few of us dead
A life as inhuman and cold as those.

THE BROADSTONE

NEAR FINVOY, COUNTY ANTRIM

We climbed by the old quarries to the wide highland of heath,
On the slope of a swale a giant dolmen,
Three heavy basalt pillars upholding the enormous slab,
Towers and abides as if time were nothing.
The hard stones are hardly dusted with lichen in nobody knows
What ages of autumns in this high solitude
Since a recordless tribe of an unknown race lifted them up
To be the availing hero's memorial,
And temple of his power. They gathered their slighter dead
    from the biting
Winds of time in his lee, the wide moor
About him is swollen with barrows and breaks upon many
    stones,
Lean gray guardians of old urned ashes,
In waves on waves of purple heather and blithe spray of its
    bells.
Here lies the hero, more than half God,
And nobody knows his name nor his race, in the bee-bright
    necropolis,
With the stone circle and his tribe around him.
Sometimes perhaps (but who'd confess it?) in soft adolescence
We used to wonder at the world, and have wished
To hear some final harmony resolve the discords of life?
—Here they are all perfectly resolved.

THE GIANT'S RING

BALLYLESSON, NEAR BELFAST

Whoever is able will pursue the plainly
False immortality of not having lived in vain but leaving some
    mark in the world.
Secretly mocking at his own insanity
He labors the same, he knows that no dead man's lip was ever
    curled in self-scorn,
And immortality is for the dead.
Jesus and Cæsar out of the bricks of man's weakness,
    Washington out of the brittle
Bones of man's strength built their memorials,
This nameless chief of a knot of forgotten tribes in the Irish
    darkness used faithfuller
Simpler materials: to diadem a hilltop
That sees the long loughs and the Mourne Mountains, with a
    ring of enormous embankment, and to build
In the center that great toad of a dolmen
Piled up of ponderous basalt that sheds the centuries like
    raindrops. He drove the labor,
And has earmarked already some four millenniums.
His very presence is here, thick-bodied and brutish, a brutal and
    senseless will-power.
Immortality? While Homer and Shakespeare are names,
Not of men but verses, and the elder has not lived nor the
    younger will not, such treadings of time.
—Conclude that secular like Christian immortality's
Too cheap a bargain: the name, the work or the soul: glass
    beads are the trade for savages.

IN THE HILL AT NEW GRANGE

ONE OF THE THREE GREAT PREHISTORIC BURIAL MOUNDS ON THE RIVER BOYNE

Who is it beside me, who is here beside me, in the hollow hill?"
A foreigner I am. "You've dug for nothing. The Danes were
    here
A thousand years before you and robbed me of my golden
    bracelets,
Stinking red-haired men from the sea, with torches and
    swords."
Dead king, you keep a better treasure than bracelets,
The peace of the dead is dearer than gold, no one can rob
    you.

What do you watch, old king, from the cave? "In the north the
    muddy chippers of flint on the Antrim coast,
Their chests covered with hair and filth, shrewd eyes under
    bushes of brow, clicking the flints together.
How we used to hate those hunters. One squats in a
    cave-mouth and makes an axe, one in a dune shapes
    bolt-heads."
They have all (and we too, old king) been dead for thousands of
    years. I see in the north a red-haired woman
Meeting her lover by Shane O'Neill's cairn, her peasant
    husband is drunk at home, she drifts up the hill
In the sleeve of twilight. "Mary Byrnes is that you?" "Ye may
    kiss a hure but not name her. Ah, lad, come down.

When I was a wee maid I used to be loving Jesus,

All helpless and bleeding on the big cross. I'd never have
    married my drunkard only the cart ran over him.

He lay helpless and bleeding in the black lane. Och, laddie, not
    here now.

Carry me up to the cairn: a man lies bloodily under the sharp
    black stones, I love that man."

Mary Byrnes, when her lover has done and finished, before he
    stands up

To button his clothes together, runs a knife in his throat. "Oh
    Shane O'Neill it's you I was loving,

Never one else. You helpless and bleeding under the stones.

Do ye weary of stretching quiet the four long centuries? Take
    this lad's blood to hearten you, it drops through the
    stones.

Drips, drops in the stones.

Drink, Shane; drink, dear: who cares if a hure is hanged? We
    kill each other in Ireland to pleasure the dead."

Great upright stones higher than the height of a man are our
    walls,

Huge overlapping stones are the summer clouds in our sky.

The hill of boulders is heaped over all. Each hundred years

One of the enormous stones will move an inch in the dark.

Each double century one of the oaks on the crown of the
    mound

Above us breaks in a wind, an oak or an ash grows.

"I see in the south Cloyne round tower burning: the Christians
    have built a spire, the thieves from the sea have burnt it,

The happy flame streams roaring up the stone tube and breaks
   from the four windows below the stone roof
Like four bright banners.
The holy men scream in their praying, the golden reliquaries are
   melted, the bell falls clanging."
They have all (and we, too, old king) been dead for a thousand
   years. I see on the island mountain Achill,
In the west where wave after wave of the beaten tribes ran up
   and starved, an old woman, her head
Covered with a shawl, sits on Slieve Mor. Two thin sharp tears
   like knives in the yellow grooves of her face,
"My cow has died," she says, "and my son forgets me." She
   crouches and starves, in the quivering Atlantic wind,
Among the great skulls of quartz on the Achill mountain.

What do you watch, old king, from the cave? "A cause of
   mighty laughter in the mound on the hill at Dundalk.
They piled the earth on the blood of one of their spitfire
   princes, their bold watchdog of the Ulster border.
After two handfuls of centuries
One Bruce, a younger drinker of battles, bloodily ceasing to be
   king of Ireland was buried above him.
Now a rich merchant has built his house on the mound's head,
   a living man. The old capon perches there trembling,
The young men of Ireland are passionate again, it is bad for a
   man of peace to have built on the hill of battles,
Oh his dear skin, Oh the papers of his wealth.
Cuchulain looks up at Bruce and Bruce at the sweating
   merchant. By God if we dead that watch the living
Could open our mouths, the earth would be split with
   laughter."

I hear like a hum in the ground the Boyne running through the
     aging
Fields forever, and one of our great blue spiral-cut stones
Settle in the dark a hair's breadth under the burden of the hill.
"We hear from cairn to cromlech all over Ireland the dead
Whisper and conspire, and whinnies of laughter tinkle in the
     raths.
The living dream but the dead are awake."

High in Donegal, in the bitter waste north, where miles on
     miles of black heather dwindle to the Bloody Foreland,
Walks an old priest, near crazy with solitude and his peasants
     like cattle, he has wrestled with his mental Satan
Half his lifetime, and endured and triumphed. He feels the
     reward suddenly await him, the churchyard wall
Looks light and faint, the slabs and mounds by the entrance. In
     the midst of mass the crucified image trembles
Above the altar, and favorably smiles. Then Father O'Donnel
Gabbles the Latin faster to an end and turns himself once more
     and says to the people, "Go home now.
Missa est." In the empty church he screams and spits on the
     Christ,
He strikes it with his hand. Well done, old priest. "Is the man
     on the cross his God, why does he strike his God?"
Because the tortured torturer is too long dying; because the
     strain in the wounded minds of men
Leaves them no peace; but here where life is worn out men
     should have peace. He desires nothing but unconsciousness,
To slip in the black bottomless lake and be still. Time for us
     also,

Old king, although no strain so many thousands of years has
wounded our minds, time to have done
With vision, as in the world's youth with desire and deed. To
lie in the dark in the hill until the stones crumble,
And the earth and the stars suck into nothing, the wheel slopes
and returns, the beautiful burden is renewed.
For probably all the same things will be born and be beautiful
again, but blessed is the night that has no glowworm.

 ANTRIM

No spot of earth where men have so fiercely for ages of time
Fought and survived and cancelled each other,
Pict and Gael and Dane, McQuillan, Clandonnel, O'Neill,
Savages, the Scot, the Norman, the English,
Here in the narrow passage and the pitiless north, perpetual
Betrayals, relentless resultless fighting.
A random fury of dirks in the dark: a struggle for survival
Of hungry blind cells of life in the womb.
But now the womb has grown old, her strength has gone forth;
a few red carts in a fog creak flax to the dubs,
And sheep in the high heather cry hungrily that life is hard; a
plaintive peace; shepherds and peasants.

We have felt the blades meet in the flesh in a hundred
ambushes
And the groaning blood bubble in the throat;
In a hundred battles the heavy axes bite the deep bone,
The mountain suddenly stagger and be darkened.
Generation on generation we have seen the blood of boys
And heard the moaning of women massacred,
The passionate flesh and nerves have flamed like pitch-pine and
fallen
And lain in the earth softly dissolving.
I have lain and been humbled in all these graves, and mixed
new flesh with the old and filled the hollow of my mouth
With maggots and rotten dust and ages of repose. I lie here and
plot the agony of resurrection.

I wish not to lie here.
There's hardly a plot of earth not blessed for burial, but here
One might dream badly.

In beautiful seas a beautiful
And sainted island, but the dark earth so shallow on the rock
Gorged with bad meat.

Kings buried in the lee of the saint,
Kings of fierce Norway, blood-boltered Scotland, bitterly
    dreaming
Treacherous Ireland.

Imagine what delusions of grandeur,
What suspicion-agonized eyes, what jellies of arrogance and
    terror
This earth has absorbed.

SHOOTING SEASON

IN THE NORTH OF SCOTLAND

The whole countryside deployed on the hills of heather, an
    army with banners,
The beaters whoop the grouse to the butts.
Three gentlemen fling up their guns and the frightened covey is
    a few wings fewer;
Then grooms approach with the panniered horses.
The gray old moorland silence has closed like water and covered
    the gunshots.
Wave on wave goes the moor to the great
Circle of the sky; the cairn on the slope names an old battle
    and beyond are
Broad gray rocks the grave-marks of clans.
Blond Celtic warriors lair in the sky-line barrows, down toward
    the sea
Stand the tall stones of the Danish captains.
We dead that handled weapons and hunted in earnest, we old
    dead have watched
Three little living gentlemen yonder
With a bitter flavor in the grin of amusement, uneasily
    remembering our own
Old sports and delights. It is better to be dust.

At East Lulworth the dead were friendly and pitiful, I saw them
    peek from their ancient earthworks on the coast hills
At the camps of the living men in the valley, the
    army-mechanics' barracks, the roads where they try the
    tanks
And the armored cars: "We also," they say, "trembled in our
    time. We felt the world change in the rain,
Our people like yours were falling under the wheel. Great past
    and declining present are a pitiful burden
For living men; but failure is not the worm that worries the
    dead, you will not weep when you come,"
Said the soft mournful shadows on the Dorset shore. And those
    on the Rollright ridge by the time-eaten stone-circle
Said nothing and had no wish in the world, having blessedly
    aged out of humanity, stared with great eyes
White as the hollowed limestone, not caring but seeing,
    inhuman as the wind.

                    But the other ghosts were not good,
But like a moon of jackals around a sick stag.
At Zennor in the tumbled granite chaos, at Marazion and the
    angel's Mount, from the hoar tide-lines:
"Be patient, dead men, the tides of their day have turned,"
    from the stone rings of the dead huts on Dartmoor,
The prison town like a stain of dirt on the distant hill: "We not
    the last," they said, "shall be hopeless,
We not alone hunger in the rain." From Avebury in the high
    heart of England, in the ancient temple,

When all the cottages darkened themselves to sleep: "Send it
    along the ridge-ways and say it on the hilltops
That the bone is broken and the meat will fall."

                                  There was also
    a ghost of a king, his cheeks hollow as the brows
Of an old horse, was paddling his hands in the reeds of
    Dozmare Pool, in the shallow, in the rainy twilight,
Feeling for the hilt of a ruinous and rusted sword. But they said
    "Be patient a little, you king of shadows,
But only wait, they will waste like snow." Then Arthur left
    hunting for the lost sword, he grinned and stood up
Gaunt as a wolf; but soon resumed the old labor, shaking the
    reeds with his hands.

                Northeastward to Wantage
On the chalk downs the Saxon Alfred
Witlessly walks with his hands lamenting. "Who are the people
    and who are the enemy?" He says bewildered,
"Who are the living, who are the dead?" The more ancient
    dead
Watch him from the wide earthworks on White Horse Hill,
    peer from the Ridgeway barrows, goggle from the
    broken
Mound and the scattered stones in the oval wood above Ashbury.
    They whisper and exult.

                        In the north also
I saw them, from the Picts' houses in the black Caithness heather
    to the bleak stones on Culloden Moor,

The rags of lost races and beaten clans, nudging each other, the
    blue lips cracking with joy, the fleshless
Anticipatory fingers jabbing at the south. And on the Welsh
    borders
Were dead men skipping and fleering behind all the hedges. An
    island of ghosts. They seemed merry, and to feel
No pity for the great pillar of empire settling to a fall, the pride
    and the power slowly dissolving.

"Doggerel," he thought, "will do for church-wardens,
Poetry's precious enough not to be wasted,"
And rhymed it all out with a skew smile:
"Spare these stones. Curst be he that moves my bones—
Will hold the hands of masons and grave-diggers."
But why did the good man care? For he wanted quietness.
He had tasted enough life in his time
To stuff a thousand; he wanted not to swim wide
In waters, nor wander the enormous air,
Nor grow into grass, enter through the mouths of cattle
The bodies of lusty women and warriors,
But all be finished. He knew it feelingly; the game
Of the whirling circles had become tiresome.
"Annihilation's impossible, but insulated
In the church under the rhyming flagstone
Perhaps my passionate ruins may be kept off market
To the end of this age. Oh, a thousand years
Will hardly leach," he thought, "this dust of that fire."

Walking in the flat Oxfordshire fields
Where the eye can find no rock to rest on but little flints
Speckle the soil, and the million-berried hedges
Tingle with birds at evening, I saw the sombre
November day redden and go down; a flight of lapwings
Whirled in the hollow of the field, and half-tame pheasants
Cried from the trees. I remembered impatiently
How the long bronze mountain of my own coast,
Where color is no account and pathos ridiculous, the sculpture
    is all,
Breaks the arrows of the setting sun
Over the enormous mounded eyeball of ocean.

                      The soft alien twilight
Worn and weak with too much humanity hooded my mind.
Poor flourishing earth, meek-smiling slave,
If sometime the swamps return and the heavy forest, black
    beech and oak-roots
Break up the paving of London streets;
And only, as long before, on the lifted ridgeways
Few people shivering by little fires
Watch the night of the forest cover the land
And shiver to hear the wild dogs howling where the cities were,
Would you be glad to be free? I think you will never
Be glad again, so kneaded with human flesh, so humbled and
    changed.

                *   *   *

Here all's down hill and passively goes to the grave,
Asks only a pinch of pleasure between the darknesses,
Contented to think that everything has been done
That's in the scope of the race: so should I also perhaps
Dream, under the empty angel of this twilight,
But the great memory of that unhumanized world,
With all its wave of good and evil to climb yet,
Its exorbitant power to match, its heartless passion to equal,
And all its music to make, beats on the grave-mound.

NOTES TO
DESCENT TO THE DEAD

It seems hardly necessary to stipulate that the elegiac tone of these verses reflects the writer's mood, and is not meant for economic or political opinion.

Shane O'Neill's cairn and the dateless monument called Ossian's Grave stand within a couple of miles of each other on the Antrim coast.

A dolmen is a prehistoric burial-house made of great stones set on end, roofed by a slab of stone. There are many still standing in Ireland and England.

Newgrange is one of three great artificial hills, on the Boyne west of Drogheda. Passages and cells were made of megalithic stonework, decorated with designs cut in the great stones, and the hills were heaped over them. No one assigns a reasonable date to these erections. Evidently they are burial mounds, like the pyramids.

The Irish round towers are well known, of course, slender, tapering spires of stone and lime mortar, of mysterious origin, but probably belfries and towers of refuge, built between 600 and 1200 A.D. They are associated with the earliest Christian churches.

Antrim is the northeasternmost county of Ireland, only a few sea-miles from Scotland. Iona is the sacred island of the Hebrides.

Avebury is a little Wiltshire village inside a great prehistoric stone-circle and fosse. It was the religious and perhaps the political capital of southern England before Stonehenge was built, i.e., before 2000 B.C., probably. The circle and the remaining stones are greater than those at Stonehenge, but the stones were not hewn to shape. Most of them are gone now; broken up to build the village.

Dozmare Pool is in Cornwall, a little flat mere in a wide wilderness, said to be the water where the sword Excalibur was cast away when King Arthur died.

The ridgeways are ancient grass-grown roads on the ridges of the hills, used by the pre-Celtic inhabitants of England, when the lowlands were impassable swamp and forest.

FROM

THURSO'S
LANDING

THE PLACE FOR NO STORY

The coast hills at Sovranes Creek:
No trees, but dark scant pasture drawn thin
Over rock shaped like flame;
The old ocean at the land's foot, the vast
Gray extension beyond the long white violence;
A herd of cows and the bull
Far distant, hardly apparent up the dark slope;
And the gray air haunted with hawks:
This place is the noblest thing I have ever seen.
No imaginable
Human presence here could do anything
But dilute the lonely self-watchful passion.

The deer were bounding like blown leaves
Under the smoke in front of the roaring wave of the brush-fire;
I thought of the smaller lives that were caught.
Beauty is not always lovely; the fire was beautiful, the terror
Of the deer was beautiful; and when I returned
Down the black slopes after the fire had gone by, an eagle
Was perched on the jag of a burnt pine,
Insolent and gorged, cloaked in the folded storms of his
    shoulders.
He had come from far off for the good hunting
With fire for his beater to drive the game; the sky was merciless
Blue, and the hills merciless black,
The sombre-feathered great bird sleepily merciless between
    them.
I thought, painfully, but the whole mind,
The destruction that brings an eagle from heaven is better than
    mercy.

# NOVEMBER SURF

Some lucky day each November great waves awake and are
    drawn
Like smoking mountains bright from the west
And come and cover the cliff with white violent cleanness: then
    suddenly
The old granite forgets half a year's filth:
The orange-peel, eggshells, papers, pieces of clothing, the clots
Of dung in corners of the rock, and used
Sheaths that make light love safe in the evenings: all the
    droppings of the summer
Idlers washed off in a winter ecstasy:
I think this cumbered continent envies its cliff then. . . . But all
    seasons
The earth, in her childlike prophetic sleep,
Keeps dreaming of the bath of a storm that prepares up the
    long coast
Of the future to scour more than her sea-lines:
The cities gone down, the people fewer and the hawks more
    numerous,
The rivers mouth to source pure; when the two-footed
Mammal, being someways one of the nobler animals, regains
The dignity of room, the value of rareness.

The flesh of the house is heavy sea-orphaned stone, the
    imagination of the house
Is in those little clay kits of swallows
Hung in the eaves, bright wings flash and return, the heavy
    rock walls commercing
With harbors of the far hills and the high
Rills of water, the river-meadow and the sea-cloud. You have
    also, O sleepy stones,
The red, the white and the marbled pigeons
To beat the blue air over the pinewood and back again in a
    moment; and the bush-hidden
Killdeer nest against the west wall-foot,
That is fed from many strange ebbs; besides the woodful of
    finches, the shoring gulls,
The sudden attentive passages of hawks.

THE BED BY THE WINDOW

I chose the bed downstairs by the sea-window for a good
    deathbed
When we built the house; it is ready waiting,
Unused unless by some guest in a twelvemonth, who hardly
    suspects
Its latter purpose. I often regard it,
With neither dislike nor desire; rather with both, so equalled
That they kill each other and a crystalline interest
Remains alone. We are safe to finish what we have to finish;
And then it will sound rather like music
When the patient daemon behind the screen of sea-rock and sky
Thumps with his staff, and calls thrice: "Come, Jeffers."

EDISON

(OCTOBER 1931)

A great toy-maker, light-bringer, patient
Finder of powers that were promptly applied to foolish and
    mean
Purposes; a man full of benevolence,
Eager for knowledge, has dropped his tools and forgotten
    contrivance.
Why must the careful gifts of good men
Narrow the lives and erode the souls of people, as trader's
Whiskey unravels a run of savages?

NEW MEXICAN MOUNTAIN

I watch the Indians dancing to help the young corn at Taos
    pueblo. The old men squat in a ring
And make the song, the young women with fat bare arms, and
    a few shame-faced young men, shuffle the dance.

The lean-muscled young men are naked to the narrow loins,
    their breasts and backs daubed with white clay,
Two eagle-feathers plume the black heads. They dance with
    reluctance, they are growing civilized; the old men persuade
    them.

Only the drum is confident, it thinks the world has not changed;
    the beating heart, the simplest of rhythms,
It thinks the world has not changed at all; it is only a dreamer,
    a brainless heart, the drum has no eyes.

These tourists have eyes, the hundred watching the dance, white
    Americans, hungrily too, with reverence, not laughter;
Pilgrims from civilization, anxiously seeking beauty, religion,
    poetry; pilgrims from the vacuum.

People from cities, anxious to be human again. Poor show how
    they suck you empty! The Indians are emptied,
And certainly there was never religion enough, nor beauty nor
    poetry here . : . to fill Americans.

Only the drum is confident, it thinks the world has not
    changed. Apparently only myself and the strong
Tribal drum, and the rockhead of Taos mountain, remember
    that civilization is a transient sickness.

SECOND BEST

A Celtic spearman forcing the cromlech-builder's brown
    daughter;
A blond Saxon, a slayer of Britons,
Building his farm outside the village he'd burned; a Norse
Voyager, wielder of oars and a sword,
Thridding the rocks at the fjord sea-end, hungry as a hawk;
A hungry Gaelic chiefling in Ulster,
Whose blood with the Norseman's rotted in the rain on a
    heather hill:
These by the world's time were very recent
Forefathers of yours. And you are a maker of verses. The pallid
Pursuit of the world's beauty on paper,
Unless a tall angel comes to require it, is a pitiful pastime.
If, burnished new from God's eyes, an angel:
And the ardors of the simple blood showing clearly a little
    ridiculous
In this changed world:—write and be quiet.

Fair head in Antrim, long dark waves of wet heather to the
    black lips of the height
Where the old McDonnel war-chief three days of grief and
    madness raged like a storm on the precipice-head
Watching the massacre that came to Rathlin on ships, helplessly
    seeing
Unavengeable things across the thin sleeve of sea. The old
    man's anguish and burning anger were not
Even in the moment of blood and smoke
Ponderable against the tough and sombre passion of the
    headland; they were nothing; not a gannet-feather's
Weight on the rock; the mood of this black basalt has never
    turned since it cooled.

                  The most beautiful woman
Of the northern world made landfall under this cliff when she
    came to the bitter end that makes the life shine,
But the black towers of the rock were more beautiful than
    Deirdre.
Weep for the pity of lovers and the beauty of bereaved men,
    the beauty of the earth is too great to weep for.

Iron rusts, and bronze has its green sickness; while flint, the
    hard stones, flint and chalcedony,
Cut the soft stream of time as if they were made for immortal
    uses. So the two-thousand-year-old
Stone axe that Barney McKaye found in the little field his father
    was ditching kept the clear surfaces
Of having been formed quite lately. He wiped it clean on his
    sleeve, and saw, while he held it to show his father,
Between the knuckled fist on the spade-handle and the brown
    beard spattered with mud, the rounded hill
Toward the Dun River, the bay beyond, all empty of sails, and
    the cliffs of Scotland with yellow sun on them
Between two showers. His father looked at the stone. " 'Tis
    nothing: they do be callin' them thunder-stones,
I think the old people used them when short of iron." It was
    taken home to the cottage, however,
And there was lost at the foot of the mud-chinked wall, in the
    earth floor.

      In 1815
The thatch took fire after a ten-day drought; the ruin was left
    abandoned; beautiful heather
Reclaimed the field. There was a Nora McKaye who married a
    McAuley,
Visited the site of her grandsire's cottage the week before they
    sailed for America. A digging rabbit

Had scratched the flint into view again, and Nora she picked it
    up from between the nettles and took it
To remember Ireland, because it felt fine in the hand and had a
    queer shape. In Michigan it was thrown out
With some cracked cups after she died.

                                       There it was taken for a
    Huron tomahawk
By one clearing rubbish to make a garden, who gave it to his
    younger boy, who traded it for bantam eggs;
It wandered from hand to hand and George Townsend had it.
    He moved to California for his son's health
And died there. His son was a hardware merchant in Monterey,
    and displayed the stone axe beside the steel ones
In his window show, but after a time he gave it to the town
    museum. It lay dustily in harbor
Until the new museum was built, and there it lay on a shelf
    under bright glass, mislabelled
But sure of itself, intact and waiting, while storms of time
Shot by outside. The building stood up the hill by the Carmel
    road, and overlooking the city
Beheld strange growths and changes and ghastly fallings. At
    length the glass
Broke from its weary windows, then a wall fell. Young oak and
    pine grew up through the floors; an earthquake
Strewed the other walls. Earth drifted, pine-needles dropped and
    mouldered, the ruin was hidden, and all the city
Below it became a pinewood and sang in the wind.

                                         White dawn
    grew over Mount Gabilan and Toro Mountain;

A tall young woman, naked except a deerskin and her sunburnt
 hair, stooped heavily, heavy with child,
To the coals of a hoarded fire in a dry stream-course. She
 awaked them, laying lichen and twigs to catch up the flame,
And crouching found that flint axe, which winter water had
 washed from the gullied bank; she found it with joy
And hastily went up the bank. Dawn like a fruit ripened for
 sunrise;
Monterey Bay was all red and yellow like the flaring sky. The
 woman called down the gully, "Oh, Wolf!
Wolf?" He came up between two pines, saying, "You have
 scared the rabbits." His beautiful naked body
Was as dark as an Indian's, but he had blue eyes. She answered,
 "I had to tell you: I found your axe
You lost yesterday morning; it was lying by the ashes." He took
 it and said, "That's a good thing.
I was greatly afraid I'd lost it, but here it is." She said, "How
 lovely the world beginning again.
Look, dear, there comes the sun. My baby be born as quietly as
 that."

FROM
SOLSTICE

ROCK AND HAWK

Here is a symbol in which
Many high tragic thoughts
Watch their own eyes.

This gray rock, standing tall
On the headland, where the seawind
Lets no tree grow,

Earthquake-proved, and signatured
By ages of storms: on its peak
A falcon has perched.

I think, here is your emblem
To hang in the future sky;
Not the cross, not the hive,

But this; bright power, dark peace;
Fierce consciousness joined with final
Disinterestedness;

Life with calm death; the falcon's
Realist eyes and act
Married to the massive

Mysticism of stone,
Which failure cannot cast down
Nor success make proud.

LIFE FROM THE LIFELESS

Spirits and illusions have died,
The naked mind lives
In the beauty of inanimate things.

Flowers wither, grass fades, trees wilt,
The forest is burnt;
The rock is not burnt.

The deer starve, the winter birds
Die on their twigs and lie
In the blue dawns in the snow.

Men suffer want and become
Curiously ignoble; as prosperity
Made them curiously vile.

But look how noble the world is,
The lonely-flowing waters, the secret-
Keeping stones, the flowing sky.

# REARMAMENT

These grand and fatal movements toward death: the grandeur of
    the mass
Makes pity a fool, the tearing pity
For the atoms of the mass, the persons, the victims, makes it
    seem monstrous
To admire the tragic beauty they build.
It is beautiful as a river flowing or a slowly gathering
Glacier on a high mountain rock-face,
Bound to plow down a forest, or as frost in November,
The gold and flaming death-dance for leaves,
Or a girl in the night of her spent maidenhood, bleeding and
    kissing.
I would burn my right hand in a slow fire
To change the future . . . I should do foolishly. The beauty of
    modern
Man is not in the persons but in the
Disastrous rhythm, the heavy and mobile masses, the dance of
    the
Dream-led masses down the dark mountain.

# AVE CAESAR

No bitterness: our ancestors did it.

They were only ignorant and hopeful, they wanted freedom but
   wealth too.

Their children will learn to hope for a Caesar.

Or rather—for we are not aquiline Romans but soft mixed
   colonists—

Some kindly Sicilian tyrant who'll keep

Poverty and Carthage off until the Romans arrive.

We are easy to manage, a gregarious people,

Full of sentiment, clever at mechanics, and we love our luxuries.

SHINE, REPUBLIC

The quality of these trees, green height; of the sky, shining, of
     water, a clear flow; of the rock, hardness
And reticence: each is noble in its quality. The love of freedom
     has been the quality of Western man.

There is a stubborn torch that flames from Marathon to
     Concord, its dangerous beauty binding three ages
Into one time; the waves of barbarism and civilization have
     eclipsed but have never quenched it.

For the Greeks the love of beauty, for Rome of ruling; for the
     present age the passionate love of discovery;
But in one noble passion we are one; and Washington, Luther,
     Tacitus, Aeschylus, one kind of man.

And you, America, that passion made you. You were not born
     to prosperity, you were born to love freedom.
You did not say "en masse," you said "independence." But we
     cannot have all the luxuries and freedom also.

Freedom is poor and laborious; that torch is not safe but
     hungry, and often requires blood for its fuel.
You will tame it against it burn too clearly, you will hood it like
     a kept hawk, you will perch it on the wrist of Caesar.

But keep the tradition, conserve the forms, the observances, keep
the spot sore. Be great, carve deep your heel-marks.
The states of the next age will no doubt remember you, and
edge their love of freedom with contempt of luxury.

DISTANT RAINFALL

Like mourning women veiled to the feet
Tall slender rainstorms walk slowly against gray cloud along the
    far verge.
The ocean is green where the river empties,
Dull gray between the points of the headlands, purple where the
    women walk.
What do they want? Whom are they mourning?
What hero's dust in the urn between the two hands hidden in
    the veil?
Titaness after Titaness proudly
Bearing her tender magnificent sorrow at her heart, the lost
    battle's beauty.

Beyond the Sierras, and sage-brush Nevada ranges, and vast
Vulture-utopias of Utah desert,
That mountain we admired last year on our summer journey,
    the same
Rose-red pyramid glows over Silverton.
Whoever takes the rock pass from Ouray sees foaming waterfalls
And trees like green flames, like the rocks flaming
Green; and above, up the wild gorge, up the wild sky,
Incredibly blood-color around the snow-spot
The violent peak. We thought it was too theatrical to last;
But if we ship to Cape Horn, or were buying
Camels in Urga, Red Mountain would not turn pale for our
    absence.
We like dark skies and lead-color heights,
But the excellence of things is really unscrupulous, it will dare
    anything.

GRAY WEATHER

It is true that, older than man and ages to outlast him, the
    Pacific surf
Still cheerfully pounds the worn granite drum;
But there's no storm; and the birds are still, no song; no kind
    of excess;
Nothing that shines, nothing is dark;
There is neither joy nor grief nor a person, the sun's tooth
    sheathed in cloud,
And life has no more desires than a stone.
The stormy conditions of time and change are all abrogated, the
    essential
Violences of survival, pleasure,
Love, wrath and pain, and the curious desire of knowing, all
    perfectly suspended.
In the cloudy light, in the timeless quietness,
One explores deeper than the nerves or heart of nature, the
    womb or soul,
To the bone, the careless white bone, the excellence.

This woman cannot live more than one year.
Her growing death is hidden in a hopeless place,
Her death is like a child growing in her,
And she knows it, you see it shine in her face.
She looks at her own hands and thinks "In a year
These will be burnt like rags in the crematory.
I shall not feel it. Where I? Where I? Not anywhere."
It is strange, it gives to her face a kind of glory.
Her mind used to be lazy and heavy her face,
Now she talks all in haste, looks young and lean
And eager, her eyes glitter with eagerness,
As if she were newly born and had never seen
The beauty of things, the terror, pain, joy, the song.
—Or is it better to live at ease, dully and long?

LOVE THE WILD SWAN

"I hate my verses, every line, every word.
Oh pale and brittle pencils ever to try
One grass-blade's curve, or the throat of one bird
That clings to twig, ruffled against white sky.
Oh cracked and twilight mirrors ever to catch
One color, one glinting flash, of the splendor of things.
Unlucky hunter, Oh bullets of wax,
The lion beauty, the wild-swan wings, the storm of the wings."
—This wild swan of a world is no hunter's game.
Better bullets than yours would miss the white breast,
Better mirrors than yours would crack in the flame.
Does it matter whether you hate your . . . self? At least
Love your eyes that can see, your mind that can
Hear the music, the thunder of the wings. Love the wild swan.

RETURN

A little too abstract, a little too wise,
It is time for us to kiss the earth again,
It is time to let the leaves rain from the skies,
Let the rich life run to the roots again.
I will go down to the lovely Sur Rivers
And dip my arms in them up to the shoulders.
I will find my accounting where the alder leaf quivers
In the ocean wind over the river boulders.
I will touch things and things and no more thoughts,
That breed like mouthless May-flies darkening the sky,
The insect clouds that blind our passionate hawks
So that they cannot strike, hardly can fly.
Things are the hawk's food and noble is the mountain, Oh
    noble
Pico Blanco, steep sea-wave of marble.

FLIGHT OF SWANS

One who sees giant Orion, the torches of winter midnight,
Enormously walking above the ocean in the west of heaven;
And watches the track of this age of time at its peak of flight
Waver like a spent rocket, wavering toward new discoveries,
Mortal examinations of darkness, soundings of depth;
And watches the long coast mountain vibrate from bronze to
     green,
Bronze to green, year after year, and all the streams
Dry and flooded, dry and flooded, in the racing seasons;
And knows that exactly this and not another is the world,
The ideal is phantoms for bait, the spirit is a flicker on a
     grave;—
May serve, with a certain detachment, the fugitive human race,
Or his own people, or his own household; but hardly himself;
And will not wind himself into hopes nor sicken with despairs.
He has found the peace and adored the God; he handles in
     autumn
The germs of far-future spring.
                         Sad sons of the stormy fall,
No escape, you have to inflict and endure; surely it is time for
     you
To learn to touch the diamond within to the diamond outside,
Thinning your humanity a little between the invulnerable
     diamonds,
Knowing that your angry choices and hopes and terrors are in
     vain,
But life and death not in vain; and the world is like a flight of
     swans.

FROM

SUCH COUNSELS
YOU GAVE ME

THE COAST-ROAD

A horseman high alone as an eagle on the spur of the mountain
    over Mirmas Canyon draws rein, looks down
At the bridge-builders, men, trucks, the power-shovels, the
    teeming end of the new coast-road at the mountain's base.
He sees the loops of the road go northward, headland beyond
    headland, into gray mist over Fraser's Point,
He shakes his fist and makes the gesture of wringing a chicken's
    neck, scowls and rides higher.

                I too
Believe that the life of men who ride horses, herders of cattle
    on the mountain pasture, plowers of remote
Rock-narrowed farms in poverty and freedom, is a good life. At
    the far end of those loops of road
Is what will come and destroy it, a rich and vulgar and
    bewildered civilization dying at the core,
A world that is feverishly preparing new wars, peculiarly vicious
    ones, and heavier tyrannies, a strangely
Missionary world, road-builder, wind-rider, educator, printer and
    picture-maker and broadcaster,
So eager, like an old drunken whore, pathetically eager to
    impose the seduction of her fled charms
On all that through ignorance or isolation might have escaped
    them. I hope the weathered horseman up yonder
Will die before he knows what this eager world will do to his
    children. More tough-minded men

Can repulse an old whore, or cynically accept her drunken
      kindnesses for what they are worth,
But the innocent and credulous are soon corrupted.

                                       Where is
      our consolation? Beautiful beyond belief
The heights glimmer in the sliding cloud, the great bronze
      gorge-cut sides of the mountain tower up invincibly,
Not the least hurt by this ribbon of road carved on their
      sea-foot.

GOING TO HORSE FLATS

Amazingly active a toothless old man
Hobbled beside me up the canyon, going to Horse Flats, he
   said,
To see to some hives of bees. It was clear that he lived alone
   and craved companionship, yet he talked little
Until we came to a place where the gorge widened, and
   deer-hunters had camped on a slip of sand
Beside the stream. They had left the usual rectangle of fired
   stones and ashes, also some crumpled
Sheets of a recent newspaper with loud headlines. The old man
   rushed at them
And spread them flat, held them his arm's length, squinting
   through narrowed eyelids—poor trick old eyes learn, to
   make
Lids act for lens. He read "Spain Battle. Rebels kill captives.
   City bombed Reds kill hostages. Prepare
For war Stalin warns troops." He trembled and said, "Please
   read me the little printing, I hardly ever
Get to hear news." He wrung his withered hands while I read;
   it was strange in that nearly inhuman wilderness
To see an old hollow-cheeked hermit dancing to the world's
   echoes. After I had read he said "That's enough.
They were proud and oppressed the poor and are punished
   for it; but those that punish them are full of envy and
   hatred
And are punished for it; and again the others; and again the
   others. It is so forever, there is no way out.

Only the crimes and cruelties grow worse perhaps." I said, "You
   are too hopeless. There are ways out."
He licked his empty gums with his tongue, wiped his mouth and
   said
"What ways?" I said "The Christian way: forgiveness, to forgive
   your enemies,
Give good for evil." The old man threw down the paper and
   said "How long ago did Christ live? Ah?
Have the people in Spain never heard about him? Or have the
   Russians,
Or Germans? Do you think I'm a fool?" "Well," I said to try
   him, "there's another way: extermination.
If the winning side will totally destroy its enemies, lives and
   thoughts, liquidate them, firing-squads
For the people and fire for the books and records: the feud will
   then be
Finished forever." He said justly, *"You're* the fool," picked up
   his bundle and hurried through the shadow-dapple
Of noon in the narrow canyon, his ragged coat-tails flapping
   like mad over the coonskin patch
In the seat of his trousers. I waited awhile, thinking he wished
   to be quit of company.

                     Sweet was the clear
Chatter of the stream now that our talk was hushed; the flitting
   water-ouzel returned to her stone;
A lovely snake, two delicate scarlet lines down the dark back,
   swam through the pool. The flood-battered
Trees by the stream are more noble than cathedral-columns.

do we invite the world's rancors and agonies
Into our minds though walking in a wilderness? Why did he
    want the news of the world? He could do nothing
To help nor hinder. Nor you nor I can . . . for the world. It is
    certain the world cannot be stopped nor saved.
It has changes to accomplish and must creep through agonies
    toward new discovery. It must, and it ought: the awful
    necessity
Is also the sacrificial duty. Man's world is a tragic music and is
    not played for man's happiness,
Its discords are not resolved but by other discords.

                              But for each man
There is real solution, let him turn from himself and man to
    love God. He is out of the trap then. He will remain
Part of the music, but will hear it as the player hears it.
He will be superior to death and fortune, unmoved by success
    or failure. Pity can make him weep still,
Or pain convulse him, but not to the center, and he can
    conquer them. . . . But how could I impart this knowledge
To that old man?

              Or indeed to anyone? I know that all men
    instinctively rebel against it. But yet
They will come to it at last.
Then man will have come of age; he will still suffer and still die,
    but like a God, not a tortured animal.

Ed Stiles and old Tom Birnam went up to their cattle on the
bare hills
Above Mal Paso; they'd ridden under the stars' white death,
when they reached the ridge the huge tiger-lily
Of a certain cloud-lapped astonishing autumn sunrise opened all
its petals. Ed Stiles pulled in his horse,
That flashy palomino he rode—cream-color, heavy white mane,
white tail, his pride—and said
"Look, Tom. My God. Ain't that a beautiful sunrise?" Birnam
drew down his mouth, set the hard old chin,
And whined: "Now, Ed: listen here: I haven't an ounce of
poetry in all my body. It's cows we're after."
Ed laughed and followed; they began to sort the heifers out of
the herd. One red little deer-legged creature
Rolled her wild eyes and ran away down the hill, the old man
hard after her. She ran through a deep-cut gully,
And Birnam's piebald would have made a clean jump but the
clay lip
Crumbled under his take-off, he slipped and
Spilled in the pit, flailed with four hooves and came out
scrambling. Stiles saw them vanish,
Then the pawing horse and the flapping stirrups. He rode and
looked down and saw the old man in the gully-bottom
Flat on his back, most grimly gazing up at the sky. He saw the
earth banks, the sparse white grass,
The strong dark sea a thousand feet down below, red with
reflections of clouds. He said "My God,

Tom, are you hurt?" Who answered slowly, "No, Ed.
I'm only lying here thinking o' my four sons"—biting the words
Carefully between his lips—"big handsome men, at present
lolling in bed in their . . . silk . . . pyjamas . . .
And why the devil I keep on working?" He stood up slowly and
wiped the dirt from his cheek, groaned, spat,
And climbed up the clay bank. Stiles laughed: "Tom, I can't tell
you: I guess you like to. By God I guess
You like the sunrises." The old man growled in his throat and
said
"Catch me my horse."

                      This old man died last winter, having
lived eighty-one years under open sky,
Concerned with cattle, horses and hunting, no thought nor
emotion that all his ancestors since the ice-age
Could not have comprehended. I call that a good life; narrow,
but vastly better than most
Men's lives, and beyond comparison more beautiful; the
wind-struck music man's bones were moulded to be the
harp for.

Our sardine fishermen work at night in the dark of the moon;
    daylight or moonlight
They could not tell where to spread the net, unable to see the
    phosphorescence of the shoals of fish.
They work northward from Monterey, coasting Santa Cruz; off
    New Year's Point or off Pigeon Point
The look-out man will see some lakes of milk-color light on the
    sea's night-purple; he points, and the helmsman
Turns the dark prow, the motorboat circles the gleaming shoal
    and drifts out her seine-net. They close the circle
And purse the bottom of the net, then with great labor haul it
    in.

                                      I cannot tell you
How beautiful the scene is, and a little terrible, then, when the
    crowded fish
Know they are caught, and wildly beat from one wall to the
    other of their closing destiny the phosphorescent
Water to a pool of flame, each beautiful slender body sheeted
    with flame, like a live rocket
A comet's tail wake of clear yellow flame; while outside the
    narrowing
Floats and cordage of the net great sea-lions come up to watch,
    sighing in the dark; the vast walls of night
Stand erect to the stars.

Lately I was looking from a night mountain-top
On a wide city, the colored splendor, galaxies of light: how
    could I help but recall the seine-net
Gathering the luminous fish? I cannot tell you how beautiful the
    city appeared, and a little terrible.
I thought, We have geared the machines and locked all together
    into interdependence; we have built the great cities; now
There is no escape. We have gathered vast populations
    incapable of free survival, insulated
From the strong earth, each person in himself helpless, on all
    dependent. The circle is closed, and the net
Is being hauled in. They hardly feel the cords drawing, yet they
    · shine already. The inevitable mass-disasters
Will not come in our time nor in our children's, but we and
    our children
Must watch the net draw narrower, government take all
    powers—or revolution, and the new government
Take more than all, add to kept bodies kept souls—or anarchy,
    the mass-disasters.

These things are Progress;
Do you marvel our verse is troubled or frowning, while it keeps
    its reason? Or it lets go, lets the mood flow
In the manner of the recent young men into mere hysteria,
    splintered gleams, crackled laughter. But they are quite
    wrong.
There is no reason for amazement: surely one always knew that
    cultures decay, and life's end is death.

THE GREAT SUNSET

A flight of six heavy-motored bombing-planes
Went over the beautiful inhuman ridges a straight course
    northward; the incident stuck itself in my memory
More than a flight of band-tail pigeons might have done
Because those wings of man and potential war seemed really
    intrusive above the remote canyon.
They changed it; I cannot say they profaned it, but the memory
All day remained like a false note in familiar music, and
    suggested no doubt
The counter-fantasy that came to my eyes in the evening, on the
    ocean cliff.

            I came from the canyon twilight
Exactly at sunset to the open shore, and felt like a sudden
    extension of consciousness the wild free light
And biting north-wind. The cloud-sky had lifted from the
    western horizon and left a long yellow panel
Between the slate-edge ocean and the eyelid cloud; the smoky
    ball of the sun rolled on the sea-line
And formless bits of vapor flew across, but when the sun was
    down
The panel of clear sky brightened, the rags of moving cloud
    took memorable shapes, dark on the light,
Whether I was dreaming or not, they became spears and
    war-axes, horses and sabres, gaunt battle-elephants
With towered backs; they became catapults and siege-guns,
    high-tilted howitzers, long tractors, armored and turreted;

They became battleships and destroyers, and great fleets of
    warplanes . . . all the proud instruments
Of man imposing his will upon weaker men: they were like a
    Roman triumph, but themselves the captives,
A triumph in reverse: all the tools of victory
Whiffed away on the north-wind into a cloud like a
    conflagration, swept from the earth, no man
From this time on to exploit nor subdue any other man. I
    thought, "What a pity our kindest dreams
Are complete liars," and turned from the glowing west toward
    the cold twilight. "To be truth-bound, the neutral
Detested by all the dreaming factions, is my errand here."

The proletariat for your Messiah, the poor and many are to
    seize power and make the world new.
They cannot even conduct a strike without cunning leaders: if
    they make a revolution their leaders
Must take the power. The first duty of men in power: to defend
    their power. What men defend
To-day they will love to-morrow; it becomes theirs, their
    property. Lenin has served the revolution,
Stalin presently begins to betray it. Why? For the sake of power,
    the Party's power, the state's
Power, armed power, Stalin's power, Caesarean power.

                           This is
    not quite a new world.
The old shepherd has been known before; great and progressive
    empires have flourished before; powerful bureaucracies
Apportioned food and labor and amusement; men have been
    massed and moulded, spies have gone here and there,
The old shepherd Caesar his vicious collies, watching the flock.
    Inevitable? Perhaps, but not new.
The ages like blind horses turning a mill tread their own
    hoof-marks. Whose corn's ground in that mill?

Then what is the answer?—Not to be deluded by dreams.
To know that great civilizations have broken down into
    violence, and their tyrants come, many times before.
When open violence appears, to avoid it with honor or choose
    the least ugly faction; these evils are essential.
To keep one's own integrity, be merciful and uncorrupted and
    not wish for evil; and not be duped
By dreams of universal justice or happiness. These dreams will
    not be fulfilled.
To know this, and know that however ugly the parts appear the
    whole remains beautiful. A severed hand
Is an ugly thing, and man dissevered from the earth and stars
    and his history . . . for contemplation or in fact . . .
Often appears atrociously ugly. Integrity is wholeness, the
    greatest beauty is
Organic wholeness, the wholeness of life and things, the divine
    beauty of the universe. Love that, not man
Apart from that, or else you will share man's pitiful confusions,
    or drown in despair when his days darken.

Farther up the gorge the sea's voice fainted and ceased.
We heard a new noise far away ahead of us, vague and metallic,
    it might have been some unpleasant bird's voice
Bedded in a matrix of long silences. At length we came to a
    little cabin lost in the redwoods,
An old man sat on a bench before the doorway filing a cross-cut
    saw; sometimes he slept,
Sometimes he filed. Two or three horses in the corral by the
    streamside lifted their heads
To watch us pass, but the old man did not.

                                       In the afternoon we
    returned the same way,
And had the picture in our minds of magnificent regions of
    space and mountain not seen before. (This was
The first time that we visited Pigeon Gap, whence you look
    down behind the great shouldering pyramid-
Edges of Pico Blanco through eagle-gulfs of air to a forest basin
Where two-hundred-foot redwoods look like the pile on a
    Turkish carpet.) With such extensions of the idol-
Worshipping mind we came down the streamside. The old man
    was still at his post by the cabin doorway, but now
Stood up and stared, said angrily "Where are you camping?"
    I said "We're not camping, we're going home." He said
From his flushed heavy face, "That's the way fires get started.
    Did you come at night?" "We passed you this morning.
You were half asleep, filing a saw." "I'll kill anybody that starts
    a fire here . . ." his voice quavered

Into bewilderment . . . "I didn't see you. Kind of feeble I guess.
My temperature's a hundred and two every afternoon." "Why,
  what's the matter?" He removed his hat
And rather proudly showed us a deep healed trench in the bald
  skull. "My horse fell at the ford,
I must 'a' cracked my head on a rock. Well, sir, I can't
  remember anything till next morning.
I woke in bed the pillow was soaked with blood, the horse was
  in the corral and had had his hay,"—
Singing the words as if he had told the story a hundred times.
  To whom? To himself, probably,—
"The saddle was on the rack and the bridle on the right nail.
  What do you think of *that* now?" He passed
His hand on his bewildered forehead and said, "Unless an angel
  or something came down and did it.
A basin of blood and water by the crick, I must 'a' washed
  myself." My wife said sharply, "Have you been to a
  doctor?"
"Oh yes," he said, "my boy happened down." She said "You
  oughtn't to be alone here: are you all alone here?"
"No," he answered, "horses. I've been all over the world: right
  here is the most beautiful place in the world.
I played the piccolo in ships' orchestras." We looked at the
  immense redwoods and dark
Fern-taken slip of land by the creek, where the horses were, and
  the yuccaed hillsides high in the sun
Flaring like torches; I said "Darkness comes early here." He
  answered with pride and joy, "Two hundred and eighty-
Five days in the year the sun never gets in here.
Like living under the sea, green all summer, beautiful." My wife
  said, "How do you know your temperature's

A hundred and two?" "Eh? The doctor. He said the bone
Presses my brain, he's got to cut out a piece. I said 'All right,
     you've got to wait till it rains,
I've got to guard my place through the fire-season.' By God," he
     said joyously,
"The quail on my roof wake me up every morning, then I look
     out the window and a dozen deer
Drift up the canyon with the mist on their shoulders. Look in
     the dust at your feet, all the little hoofprints."

OH, LOVELY ROCK

We stayed the night in the pathless gorge of Ventana Creek, up
    the east fork.
The rock walls and the mountain ridges hung forest on forest
    above our heads, maple and redwood,
Laurel, oak, madrone, up to the high and slender Santa Lucian
    firs that stare up the cataracts
Of slide-rock to the star-color precipices.

                            We lay on gravel and
kept a little camp-fire for warmth.
Past midnight only two or three coals glowed red in the cooling
    darkness; I laid a clutch of dead bay-leaves
On the ember ends and felted dry sticks across them and lay
    down again. The revived flame
Lighted my sleeping son's face and his companion's, and the
    vertical face of the great gorge-wall
Across the stream. Light leaves overhead danced in the fire's
    breath, tree-trunks were seen: it was the rock wall
That fascinated my eyes and mind. Nothing strange: light-gray
    diorite with two or three slanting seams in it,
Smooth-polished by the endless attrition of slides and floods; no
    fern nor lichen, pure naked rock . . . as if I were
Seeing rock for the first time. As if I were seeing through the
    flame-lit surface into the real and bodily
And living rock. Nothing strange . . . I cannot
Tell you how strange: the silent passion, the deep nobility and
    childlike loveliness: this fate going on

Outside our fates. It is here in the mountain like a grave smiling
    child. I shall die, and my boys
Will live and die, our world will go on through its rapid agonies
    of change and discovery; this age will die,
And wolves have howled in the snow around a new Bethlehem:
    this rock will be here, grave, earnest, not passive: the
    energies
That are its atoms will still be bearing the whole mountain
    above: and I, many packed centuries ago,
Felt its intense reality with love and wonder, this lonely rock.

OCTOBER WEEK-END

It is autumn still, but at three in the morning
All the magnificent wonders of midwinter midnight, blue
  dog-star,
Orion, red Aldebaran, the ermine-fur Pleiades,
Parading above the gable of the house. Their music is their
  shining,
And the house beats like a heart with dance-music
Because our boys have grown to the age when girls are their
  music.
There is wind in the trees, and the gray ocean's
Music on the rock. I am warming my blood with starlight, not
  with girls' eyes,
But really the night is quite mad with music.

An eagle's nest on the head of an old redwood on one of the
     precipice-footed ridges
Above Ventana Creek, that jagged country which nothing but a
     falling meteor will ever plow; no horseman
Will ever ride there, no hunter cross this ridge but the winged
     ones, no one will steal the eggs from this fortress.
The she-eagle is old, her mate was shot long ago, she is now
     mated with a son of hers.
When lightning blasted her nest she built it again on the same
     tree, in the splinters of the thunderbolt.
The she-eagle is older than I; she was here when the fires of
     eighty-five raged on these ridges,
She was lately fledged and dared not hunt ahead of them but
     ate scorched meat. The world has changed in her time;
Humanity has multiplied, but not here; men's hopes and
     thoughts and customs have changed, their powers are
     enlarged,
Their powers and their follies have become fantastic,
The unstable animal never has been changed so rapidly. The
     motor and the plane and the great war have gone over
     him,
And Lenin has lived and Jehovah died: while the mother-eagle
Hunts her same hills, crying the same beautiful and lonely cry
     and is never tired; dreams the same dreams,
And hears at night the rock-slides rattle and thunder in the
     throats of these living mountains.

                                          It is good for man
To try all changes, progress and corruption, powers, peace and
    anguish, not to go down the dinosaur's way
Until all his capacities have been explored: and it is good for
    him
To know that his needs and nature are no more changed in fact
    in ten thousand years than the beaks of eagles.

The world's as the world is; the nations rearm and prepare to
    change; the age of tyrants returns;
The greatest civilization that has ever existed builds itself higher
    towers on breaking foundations.
Recurrent episodes; they were determined when the ape's
    children first ran in packs, chipped flint to an edge.

I lie and hear
        dark rain beat the roof, and the blind wind.

                In the morning perhaps
I shall find strength again
To value the immense beauty of this time of the world, the
    flowers of decay their pitiful loveliness, the fever-dream
Tapestries that back the drama and are called the future. This
    ebb of vitality feels the ignoble and cruel
Incidents, not the vast abstract order.

              I lie and hear dark rain
    beat the roof, and the night-blind wind.

In the Ventana country darkness and rain and the roar of
    waters fill the deep mountain-throats.
The creekside shelf of sand where we lay last August under a
    slip of stars,
And firelight played on the leaning gorge-walls, is drowned and
    lost. The deer of the country huddle on a ridge

In a close herd under madrone-trees; they tremble when a
    rock-slide goes down, they open great darkness-
Drinking eyes and press closer.

               Cataracts of rock
Rain down the mountain from cliff to cliff and torment the
    stream-bed. The stream deals with them. The laurels are
    wounded,
Redwoods go down with their earth and lie thwart the gorge. I
    hear the torrent boulders battering each other,
I feel the flesh of the mountain move on its bones in the wet
    darkness.

             Is this more beautiful
Than man's disasters? These wounds will heal in their time; so
    will humanity's. This is more beautiful . . . at night . . .

FROM

SELECTED POEMS

Beyond the narrows of the Inner Hebrides
We sailed the cold angry sea toward Barra, where Heaval
   mountain
Lifts like a mast. There were few people on the steamer, it was
   late in the year; I noticed most an old shepherd,
Two wise-eyed dogs wove anxious circles around his feet, and a
   thin-armed girl
Who cherished what seemed a doll, wrapping it against the
   sea-wind. When it moved I said to my wife "She'll smother
   it."
And she to the girl: "Is your baby cold? You'd better run down
   out of the wind and uncover its face."
She raised the shawl and said "He is two weeks old. His mother
   died in Glasgow in the hospital
Where he was born. She was my sister." I looked ahead at the
   bleak island, gray stones, ruined castle,
A few gaunt houses under the high and comfortless mountain;
   my wife looked at the sickly babe,
And said "There's a good doctor in Barra? It will soon be
   winter." "Ah," she answered, "Barra'd be heaven for him,
The poor wee thing, there's Heaval to break the wind. We live
   on a wee island yonder away,
Just the one house."
                      The steamer moored, and a skiff—what
   they call a curragh, like a canvas canoe
Equipped with oars—came swiftly along the side. The
   dark-haired girl climbed down to it, with one arm holding

That doubtful slip of life to her breast; a tall young man with
    sea-pale eyes and an older man
Helped her; if a word was spoken I did not hear it. They
    stepped a mast and hoisted a henna-color
Bat's wing of sail.
             Now, returned home
After so many thousands of miles of road and ocean, all the
    hulls sailed in, the houses visited,
I remember that slender skiff with dark henna sail
Bearing off across the stormy sunset to the distant island
Most clearly; and have rather forgotten the dragging whirlpools
    of London, the screaming haste of New York.

THEORY OF TRUTH

(REFERENCE TO CHAPTER II, *THE WOMEN AT POINT SUR*)

I stand near Soberanes Creek, on the knoll over the sea, west of
    the road. I remember
This is the very place where Arthur Barclay, a priest in revolt,
    proposed three questions to himself:
First, is there a God and of what nature? Second, whether
    there's anything after we die but worm's meat?
Third, how should men live? Large time-worn questions no
    doubt; yet he touched his answers, they are not
    unattainable;
But presently lost them again in the glimmer of insanity.

                                How
    many minds have worn these questions; old coins
Rubbed faceless, dateless. The most have despaired and accepted
    doctrine; the greatest have achieved answers, but always
With aching strands of insanity in them.

I think of Lao-tze; and the dear beauty of the Jew whom they
    crucified but he lived, he was greater than Rome;
And godless Buddha under the boh-tree, straining through his
    mind the delusions and miseries of human life.

Why does insanity always twist the great answers?
                                Because only
    tormented persons want truth.

Man is an animal like other animals, wants food and success
    and women, not truth. Only if the mind
Tortured by some interior tension has despaired of happiness:
    then it hates its life-cage and seeks further,
And finds, if it is powerful enough. But instantly the private
    agony that made the search
Muddles the finding.
                        Here was a man who envied the chiefs of
    the provinces of China their power and pride,
And envied Confucius his fame for wisdom. Tortured by hardly
    conscious envy he hunted the truth of things,
Caught it, and stained it through with his private impurity. He
    praised inaction, silence, vacancy: why?
Because the princes and officers were full of business, and wise
    Confucius of words.

Here was a man who was born a bastard, and among the people
That more than any in the world valued race-purity, chastity,
    the prophetic splendors of the race of David.
Oh intolerable wound, dimly perceived. Too loving to curse his
    mother, desert-driven, devil-haunted,
The beautiful young poet found truth in the desert, but found
    also
Fantastic solution of hopeless anguish. The carpenter was not
    his father? Because God was his father,
Not a man sinning, but the pure holiness and power of God.
    His personal anguish and insane solution
Have stained an age; nearly two thousand years are one vast
    poem drunk with the wine of his blood.

And here was another Saviour, a prince in India,
A man who loved and pitied with such intense comprehension
     of pain that he was willing to annihilate
Nature and the earth and stars, life and mankind, to annul the
     suffering. He also sought and found truth,
And mixed it with his private impurity, the pity, the denials.

                                              Then
     search for truth is foredoomed and frustrate?
Only stained fragments?

                    Until the mind has turned its love from
     itself and man, from parts to the whole.

PRESCRIPTION OF PAINFUL ENDS

Lucretius felt the change of the world in his time, the great
    republic riding to the height
Whence every road leads downward; Plato in his time watched
    Athens
Dance the down path. The future is a misted landscape, no man
    sees clearly, but at cyclic turns
There is a change felt in the rhythm of events, as when an
    exhausted horse
Falters and recovers, then the rhythm of the running hoof-beats
    is changed: he will run miles yet,
But he must fall: we have felt it again in our own lifetime, slip,
    shift and speed-up
In the gallop of the world; and now perceive that, come peace
    or war, the progress of Europe and America
Becomes a long process of deterioration—starred with famous
    Byzantiums and Alexandrias,
Surely—but downward. One desires at such times
To gather the insights of the age summit against future loss,
    against the narrowing mind and the tyrants,
The pedants, the mystagogues, the barbarians: one builds poems
    for treasuries, time-conscious poems: Lucretius
Sings his great theory of natural origins and of wise conduct;
    Plato smiling carves dreams, bright cells
Of incorruptible wax to hive the Greek honey.

                               Our own time,
    much greater and far less fortunate,

Has acids for honey, and for fine dreams
The immense vulgarities of misapplied science and decaying
     Christianity: therefore one christens each poem, in dutiful
Hope of burning off at least the top layer of the time's
     uncleanness, from the acid-bottles.

COME, LITTLE BIRDS

I paid the woman what she asked, and followed her down to
    the water side, and her two sons
Came down behind us; one of them brought a spade, the other
    led the black calf and tied him up short
To a sycamore trunk over the stream-bank. It was near the foot
    of the mountain, where the Sur River
Pours from its gorge, foaming among great stones; and evening
    had come
But the light was still clear. The old woman brought us to a
    tongue of grassed land under the stream-bank;
One of her boys gathered dry sticks for a fire, the other cleared
    and repaired a short shallow trench
That scored the earth there; then they heaped up the sticks and
    made yellow flame, about ten feet from the trench
On the north side, right against the water; the woman sat
    opposite the fire and facing it, gazing northward,
Her back against a big stone.
                          She closed her eyes and hummed
    tuneless music, nodding her vulturine head
To the dull rhythm; through which one heard the fire snoring
    and the river flowing, and the surf on the shore
Over the hill. After some time she widened her eyes, and their
    sight was rolled up
Under her forehead, I saw the firelight
Flicker on the blank whites; she raised her arms and cried out
In a loud voice. Instantly her two boys went up and fetched the
    black calf though he plunged and struggled.

They tied his hind feet with a tight knot, and passed the bight
    of the rope over a sycamore bough
That hung above the stream and the head of the trench; they
    tugged his hind feet up to it, so that he fell
On the knees of his forelegs over the trench-head. Then one of
    the two young men sheared the calf's throat
With a sharp knife, holding him by one ear, the other by an ear
    and the nostrils, and the blood spouted
Into the furrow. The woman, her body twitching convulsively,
    "Come, little birds."
She screamed through her tightened throat like a strangling
    person,
"Put on the life, here is the blood, come, you gray birds."

                        By this time deep night had come,
And the fire down to red coals; there was a murmur along the
    stream-side as if a sea-wind were moving
Through the dark forest; then I saw dimly in the light of the
    coals the steam that climbed the cold air
From the hot blood and hung stagnant above the trench
Stirred, as if persons were stooping through it and stirring it;
    and distant whispers began to hiss in the trench,
And gray shapes moved. One said, wiry-thin: "Out of my way,
    you dregs." Another answered, "Stand back.
You've had your turn."

                    These were no doubt the souls of the
    dead, that dark-eyed woman
Had promised would come and tell me what I had to know:
    they looked rather like starlight sheep,

That were driven through the dust all day and deep night has
    come, they huddle at a bend of the lane, scared by the
    dogs,
Gray and exhausted, and if one goes under the others trample
    him.

                                One of the old woman's boys
Gradually revived the spent fire with dry leaves and twigs, so
    that the light increased imperceptibly,
Yet many of that whispering flock were frightened away. Those
    that remained, several still greedy cowered
Over the blood-trench, others erect wavered like long pale
    water-weeds; I went near them,
They sighed and whispered, leaning away from me like rooted
    water-weeds. I said, "if you are the souls of the dead,
And this old woman's trance and the warm blood make you
    able to answer—" and I was about to say,
"Then tell me what death is like: is it sleep or waking, captivity
    or freedom, dreams or reality?"—but they
Hearing my thought whispered, "We know, we know, we know,"
    wavering like water-weeds; then one leaned toward me,
Saying, "Tell my mother." "What?" I said. "Tell her I was well
    enough
Before that old buzzard waked me. I died in the
    base-hospital—" Another of the forms crossed him and
    said
"God curse every man that makes war or plans it." (This was in
    nineteen twenty, about two years
After the Armistice.) "God curse every Congressman that voted
    it. God curse Wilson." His face like an axe

Passed between my eyes and the fire and he entered the
    darkness beyond the light-rim. I asked the other,
"What is your mother's name?" But he could not answer, but
    only stared at me. I said, "Does she live on the Coast
Or in Monterey?" He stared at me and struck his forehead and
    stood aside.

            Others came toward me, two of whom
Seemed to be women; but now I saw a known form, tall, gaunt,
    gray-haired, and the shoulders so stooped
They appeared like a hump; he leaned to the fire, warming his
    gray old hands. I avoided the other
Shapes of the dead and went to him; my heart was shaking
And my eyes wet. "Father," I said. He answered clearly, "Is that
    you, Robin?" I said, "Father,
Forgive me. I dishonored and wasted all your hopes of me, one
    by one; yet I loved you well."
He smiled calmly and answered, "I suppose hope is a folly. We
    often learn that
Before we die. We learn," he said, "nothing afterwards." Then I
    was silent, and breathed and asked,
"Is it a sleep?" "With a dream sometimes. But far too bloodless
    to grieve," he said, "or gladden the dreamer;
And soon, I conjecture, even this pin's weight and echo of
    consciousness that makes me speak to you
Will dissolve in the stream." He smiled and rubbed his gray
    hands together and said, "Amen. If you come
To Endor again I shall not be present." Then I wished to tell
    him
Our little news: that his name would continue in the world, for
    we had two sons now; and that my mother and my brother

Were well; and also the outcome of the great war, because he
    had died
In its fifth month. He was patient and let me speak, but clearly
    not cared at all.

                    Meanwhile the woman
Had been groaning in her trance; I noticed the shapes of the
    dead changed with her breathing: when she drew breath
They became stronger, when her breath was delayed they grew
    faint and vague. But now she became exhausted, her
    breathing
Was like a death-rattle, with terrifying pauses between the gasps.
    One of her boys ran to restore her;
The other heaped the fire high, and the pale dead
Were fleeing away; but a certain one of them came running
    toward me, slender and naked, I saw the firelight
Glitter on her bare thighs; she said, "I am Tamar Cauldwell
    from Lobos: write my story. Tell them
I have my desire." She passed me and went like a lamp through
    the dark wood.
                    This was all. The young men
Carried their mother up to the cabin; I was left alone and
    stayed by the fire all night, studying
What I had heard and seen, until yellow dawn stood over the
    mountain.

                    This was all? I thought not.
I thought these decaying shadows and echoes of personality are
    only a by-play; they are not the spirit
That we see in one loved, or in saint or hero,

Shining through flesh. And I have seen it shine from a
  mountain through rock, and even from an old tree
Through the tough bark. The spirit (to call it so: what else
  could I call it?) is not a personal quality, and not
Mortal; it comes and goes, never dies. It is not to be found in
  death: dredge not the shadow-world. The dead
Have no news for us. We have for them, but they do not care.
  Peace to them.

CONTEMPLATION OF THE SWORD

(APRIL 1938)

Reason will not decide at last; the sword will decide.

The sword: an obsolete instrument of bronze or steel, formerly
>   used to kill men, but here

In the sense of a symbol. The sword: that is: the storms and
>   counter-storms of general destruction; killing of men,

Destruction of all goods and materials; massacre, more or less
>   intentional, of children and women;

Destruction poured down from wings, the air made accomplice,
>   the innocent air

Perverted into assassin and poisoner.

The sword: that is: treachery and cowardice, incredible baseness,
>   incredible courage, loyalties, insanities.

The sword: weeping and despair, mass-enslavement,
>   mass-torture, frustration of all the hopes

That starred man's forehead. Tyranny for freedom, horror for
>   happiness, famine for bread, carrion for children.

Reason will not decide at last, the sword will decide.

Dear God, who are the whole splendor of things and the sacred
>   stars, but also the cruelty and greed, the treacheries

And vileness, insanities and filth and anguish: now that this
>   thing comes near us again I am finding it hard

To praise you with a whole heart.

>   I know what pain is, but pain
>   can shine. I know what death is, I have sometimes

Longed for it. But cruelty and slavery and degradation,
    pestilence, filth, the pitifulness
Of men like little hurt birds and animals . . . if you were only
Waves beating rock, the wind and the iron-cored earth, the
    flaming insolent wildness of sun and stars,
With what a heart I could praise your beauty.
                                    You will not repent, nor
    cancel life, nor free man from anguish
For many ages to come. You are the one that tortures himself
    to discover himself: I am
One that watches you and discovers you, and praises you in
    little parables, idyl or tragedy, beautiful
Intolerable God.
                    The sword: that is:
I have two sons whom I love. They are twins, they were born in
    nineteen sixteen, which seemed to us a dark year
Of a great war, and they are now of the age
That war prefers. The first-born is like his mother, he is so
    beautiful
That persons I hardly know have stopped me on the street to
    speak of the grave beauty of the boy's face.
The second-born has strength for his beauty; when he strips for
    swimming the hero shoulders and wrestler loins
Make him seem clothed. The sword: that is: loathsome
    disfigurements, blindness, mutilation, locked lips of boys
Too proud to scream.
                    Reason will not decide at last: the sword
    will decide.

THE DAY IS A POEM

(SEPTEMBER 19, 1939)

This morning Hitler spoke in Danzig, we heard his voice.
A man of genius: that is, of amazing
Ability, courage, devotion, cored on a sick child's soul,
Heard clearly through the dog wrath, a sick child
Wailing in Danzig; invoking destruction and wailing at it.
Here, the day was extremely hot; about noon
A south wind like a blast from hell's mouth spilled a slight rain
On the parched land, and at five a light earthquake
Danced the house, no harm done. Tonight I have been amusing
    myself
Watching the blood-red moon droop slowly
Into black sea through bursts of dry lightning and distant
    thunder.
Well: the day is a poem: but too much
Like one of Jeffers's, crusted with blood and barbaric omens,
Painful to excess, inhuman as a hawk's cry.

FROM

THE DOUBLE AXE

PEARL HARBOR

I

Here are the fireworks. The men who conspired and labored
To embroil this republic in the wreck of Europe have got their
        bargain—
And a bushel more. As for me, what can I do but fly the
        national flag from the top of the tower?
America has neither race nor religion nor its own language:
        nation or nothing.
                        Stare, little tower,
Confidently across the Pacific, the flag on your head. I built you
        at the other war's end,
And the sick peace; I based you on living rock, granite on
        granite; I said, "Look, you gray stones:
Civilization is sick: stand awhile and be quiet and drink the
        sea-wind, you will survive
Civilization."
                        But now I am old, and O stones be modest. Look,
        little tower:
This dust blowing is only the British Empire; these torn leaves
        flying
Are only Europe; the wind is the plane-propellers; the smoke is
        Tokyo. The child with the butchered throat
Was too young to be named. Look no farther ahead.

II

The war that we have carefully for years provoked
Catches us unprepared, amazed and indignant. Our warships
        are shot

Like sitting ducks and our planes like nest-birds, both our coasts
   ridiculously panicked,
And our leaders make orations. This is the people
That hopes to impose on the whole planetary world
An American peace.
                        (Oh, we'll not lose our war: my money on
   amazed Gulliver
And his horse-pistols.)
                        Meanwhile our prudent officers
Have cleared the coast-long ocean of ships and fishing-craft, the
   sky of planes, the windows of light: these clearings
Make a great beauty. Watch the wide sea; there is nothing
   human; its gulls have it. Watch the wide sky
All day clean of machines; only at dawn and dusk one military
   hawk passes
High on patrol. Walk at night in the black-out,
The firefly lights that used to line the long shore
Are all struck dumb; shut are the shops, mouse-dark the houses.
   Here the prehuman dignity of night
Stands, as it was before and will be again. O beautiful
Darkness and silence, the two eyes that see God; great staring
   eyes.

INK-SACK

The squid, frightened or angry, shoots darkness
Out of her ink-sack; the fighting destroyer throws out a
     smoke-screen;
And fighting governments produce lies.
But squid and warship do it to confuse the enemy, governments
Mostly to stupefy their own people.
It might be better to let the roof burn and the walls crash
Than save a nation with floods of excrement.

Calm and full the ocean under the cool dark sky; quiet rocks
     and the birds fishing; the night-herons
Have flown home to their wood . . . while east and west in
     Europe and Asia and the islands unimaginable agonies

Consume mankind. Not a few thousand but uncounted millions,
     not a day but years, pain, horror, sick hatred;
Famine that dries the children to little bones and huge eyes;
     high explosive that fountains dirt, flesh and bone-splinters.

Sane and intact the seasons pursue their course, autumn slopes
     to December, the rains will fall
And the grass flourish, with flowers in it: as if man's world were
     perfectly separate from nature's, private and mad.

But that's not true; even the P-38s and the Flying Fortresses are
     as natural as horse-flies;
It is only that man, his griefs and rages, are not what they seem
     to man, not great and shattering, but really

Too small to produce any disturbance. This is good. This is the
     sanity, the mercy. It is true that the murdered
Cities leave marks in the earth for a certain time, like fossil
     rain-prints in shale, equally beautiful.

HISTORICAL CHOICE

(WRITTEN IN 1943)

Strong enough to be neutral—as is now proved, now American
    power
From Australia to the Aleutian fog-seas, and Hawaii to Africa,
    rides every wind—we were misguided
By fraud and fear, by our public fools and a loved leader's
    ambition,
To meddle in the fever-dreams of decaying Europe. We could
    have forced peace, even when France fell; we chose
To make alliance and feed war.

                             Actum est. There is no returning now.
Two bloody summers from now (I suppose) we shall have to
    take up the corrupting burden and curse of victory.
We shall have to hold half the earth; we shall be sick with
    self-disgust,
And hated by friend and foe, and hold half the earth—or let it
    go, and go down with it. Here is a burden
We are not fit for. We are not like Romans and
    Britons—natural world-rulers,
Bullies by instinct—but we have to bear it. Who has kissed Fate
    on the mouth, and blown out the lamp—must lie with her.

WAR-GUILT TRIALS

(NOVEMBER 1945)

The mumble-jumble drones on, the hangman waits; the shabby
  surviving
Leaders of Germany are to learn that *Vae Victis*
Means *Weh den Besiegten.* This kind of thing may console the
  distresses
Of Europeans: but for *us!*—Also we've caught
A poet, a small shrill man like a twilight bat,
Accused of being a traitor to his country. I have a bat in my
  tower
That knows more about treason, and about her country.

ORCA

Sea-lions loafed in the swinging tide in the inlet, long fluent
  creatures
Bigger than horses, and at home in their element
As if the Pacific Ocean had been made for them. Farther off
  shore the island-rocks
Bristled with quiet birds, gulls, cormorants, pelicans, hundreds
  and thousands
Standing thick as grass on a cut of turf. Beyond these, blue,
  gray, green, wind-straked, the ocean
Looked vacant; but then I saw a little black sail
That left a foam-line; while I watched there were two of them,
  two black triangles, tacking and veering, converging
Toward the rocks and the shore. I knew well enough
What they were: the dorsal fins of two killer-whales: but how
  the sea-lions
Low-floating within the rock-throat knew it, I know not.
  Whether they heard or they smelled them, suddenly
They were in panic; and some swam for the islands, others
Blindly along the granite banks of the inlet; one of them, more
  pitiful, scrabbled the cliff
In hope to climb it: at that moment black death drove in,
Silently like a shadow into the sea-gorge. It had the shape, the
  size, and it seemed the speed
Of one of those flying vipers with which the Germans lashed
  London. The water boiled for a moment
And nothing seen; and at the same moment

The birds went up from the islands, the soaring gulls, laborious
    pelicans, arrowy cormorants, a screaming
And wheeling sky. Meanwhile, below me, brown blood and
    foam
Striped the water of the inlet.

                        Here was death, and with terror,
    yet it looked clean and bright, it was beautiful.
Why? Because there was nothing human involved, suffering nor
    causing; no lies, no smirk and no malice;
All strict and decent; the will of man had nothing to do here.
    The earth is a star, its human element
Is what darkens it. War is evil, the peace will be evil, cruelty is
    evil; death is not evil. But the breed of man
Has been queer from the start. It looks like a botched
    experiment that has run wild and ought to be stopped.

FROM

HUNGERFIELD

If time is only another dimension, then all that dies
Remains alive; not annulled, but removed
Out of our sight. Una is still alive.
A few years back we are making love, greedy as hawks,
A boy and a married girl. A few years back
We are still young, strong-shouldered, joyfully laboring
To make our house. Then she, in the wide sea-window,
Endlessly enduring but not very patient,
Teaches our sons to read. She is still there,
Her beautiful pale face, heavy hair, great eyes
Bent to the book. And a few years back
We sit with our grown sons in the pitching motor-boat
Off Horn Head in Donegal, watching the sea-parrots
Tumble like clowns along the thousand-foot cliff, and the
    gannets like falling stars
Hawk at the sea: her great blue eyes are brimmed
With the wild beauty. Or we walk in Orkney,
Under the mystery of huge stones that stand there,
Raised high in the world's dawn by unknown men to forgotten
    gods,
And see dimly through the deep northern dusk

A great skein of wild swans drop from the cloud
To the gray lake. She weeps a little for joy of beauty. Only the
    homecoming
To our loved rock over the gray and ageless Pacific
Makes her such joy.

It is possible that all these conditions
of us
Are fixed points on the returning orbit of time and exist
eternally . . .
It is no good. Una has died, and I
Am left waiting for death, like a leafless tree
Waiting for the roots to rot and the trunk to fall.

I never thought you would leave me, dear love.
I knew you would die some time, I should die first—
But you have died. It is quite natural:
Because you loved life you must die first, and I
Who never cared much live on. Life is cheap, these days;
We have to compete with Asia, we are cheap as dust,
And death is cheap, but not hers. It is a common thing:
We die, we cease to exist, and are dear lovers
Fulfil themselves with sorrow and drunkenness, the quart at
midnight
And the cups in the morning—or they go seeking
A second love: but you and I are at least
Not ridiculous.

September again. The gray grass, the gray sea,
The ink-black trees with white-bellied night-herons in them,
Brawling on the boughs at dusk, barking like dogs—
And the awful loss. It is a year. She has died: and I
Have lived for a long year on soft rotten emotions,
Vain longing and drunken pity, grief and gray ashes—
Oh child of God!

It is not that I am lonely for you. I am lonely:
I am mutilated, for you were part of me:
But men endure that. I am growing old and my love is gone:
No doubt I can live without you, bitterly and well.
That's not the cry. My torment is memory
My grief to have seen the banner and beauty of your brave life
Dragged in the dust down the dim road to death. To have seen
    you defeated,
You who never despaired, passing through weakness
And pain—

                            to nothing. It is usual I believe. I stood by; I believe
I never failed you. The contemptible thought—
Whether I failed or not! *I* am not the one.
I was not dying. Is death bitter, my dearest? It is nothing.
It is a silence. But dying can be bitter.

                                        In this black year
I have thought often of Hungerfield, the man at Horse Creek,
Who fought with Death—bodily, said the witnesses, throat for
    throat,
Fury against fury in the dark—
And conquered him. If I had had the courage and the hope—
Or the pure rage—
I should be now Death's captive, no doubt, not conqueror.
I should be with my dearest, in the hollow darkness
Where nothing hurts.

                        I should not remember
Your silver-backed hand-mirror you asked me for,
And sat up in bed to gaze in it, to see your face
A little changed. You were still beautiful,

But not—as you'd been—a falcon. You said nothing; you sighed
    and laid down the glass; and I
Made a dog smile over a tearing heart,
Saying that you looked well.
                   The lies—the
    faithless hopeless unbelieved lies,
While you lay dying.
              For these reasons
I wish to make verses again, to drug memory,
To make it sleep for a moment. Never fear: I shall not forget
    you—
Until I am with you. The dead indeed forget all things.
And when I speak to you it is only play-acting
And self-indulgence: you cannot hear me, you do not exist.
    Dearest . . .

The story: Horse Creek drives blithely down its rock bed
High on the thin-turfed mountain, as we have seen it, but at
    the sea-mouth
Turns dark and fierce; black lava cliffs oppress it and it bites
    through them, the redwood trees in the gorge-throat
Are tortured dwarfs deformed by centuries of storm, broad
    trunks ancient as Caesar, and tattered heads
Hardly higher than the house. There is an angry concentration
    of power here, rock, storm and ocean;
The skies are dark, and darkness comes up like smoke
Out of the ground.
             It was here that Hungerfield sat by his
    mother's bedside,
In the great room at the house-top, under the heavy slant of the
    rafters: she had chosen this loft to lie in

Because it was as wide as the house, one could see west and
    east, ocean and mountain, from the low-silled windows
Without lifting from bed. But now her eyes were closed, she lay
    under opiate, gasping and muttering,
A tall woman, big-boned and aquiline-faced, with thin gray hair
And thin gray lips. She had been on her bed helpless for half a
    year
Like a ship on a reef.
                Hungerfield sat beside her, his great
    shoulders hunched like a vulture's.
There was nothing to do, and he felt his strength
Turn sour, unused. He had been a man of violence, and formed
    for violence, but what could violence do here?
He could not even breathe for her. She was, in fact, drowning,
    here on the bed; metastases of cancer
Had found the lungs.
                This is my wound. This is what never time
    nor change nor whiskey will heal:
To have watched the bladed throat-muscles lifting the
    breast-bone, frail strands of exhausted flesh, laboring,
    laboring
Only for a little air. The poets who sing of life without
    remembering its agony
Are fools or liars.
                Hungerfield watched the winter day's end die
    in dark fire
In the west windows. He lighted the little coal-oil lamp in its
    bracket and sat down again,
Hunched, full of helpless fury. He had fought in two so-called
    world wars, he had killed men, he knew all the tricks,
But who kills cancer?

                    He remembered when he was young, after
        his first battle,
He had met Death in a hospital. Dreamed it, no doubt, dizzy
        with ether, having three machine-gun slugs through his
        belly,
And killed some men, two of them with his hands after he was
        wounded: he had seen Death come in for him,
Into the French barn which they called a hospital. Death walked
        in human form, handsome and arrogant
Among the camp-cots, a long, dark and contemptuous face,
        emperor of all men, choosing the souls
That he would take. It was nothing horrible; it was only
        absolute power
Taking his own. He beckoned: the obedient soul
Flew into his hand. Hungerfield thought that Death was right to
        despise them, they came like slaves. He thought,
"The poor bastards are tired after a battle"—he thought in his
        own language—"and their wounds hurt,
They want relief"—but at that moment the towering dark
        power approached him and made a sign,
Such as one makes to a dog, trained but not liked,
"Come here to me." Hungerfield felt such a wave of rage
That his wounds closed their mouths; the leonine adrenal
        glands poured their blind fury
Into his blood, and the great nerves of the brain
Gave eyes to it; he was suddenly well and powerful, with
        burning eyes: "Come and try me. We'll see
Which one's the dog." Death amazed glared at him.
                    He was like the
        defeated

Roman dictator in the ruins of Carthage,
Alone, when the two soldiers found him, unarmed and
   guardless, his head worth an ass's load of gold:
He lifted his indomitable head, scowling, and they
Fled from him, like boys who have chased a rabbit in the
   bushes and find a bear. So Death stared at Hungerfield,
Death himself, with his empty black eyes and sneering
   astonished face, at such a mask of fury
That he preferred to avoid it. The blue eyes and the black ones
   fought in the air: it was Death's that failed.
He shrugged his high heavy shoulders and turned aside.
                                    "My senseless dream,"
Hungerfield thought. "The loss of blood and the dregs of ether
   made a fine dream.
How I wish it were true." He looked at his mother's face,
   gasping and drained, and the thin lips
Black in the half-light. She had enormous vitality, he hoped she
   was not conscious. He heard light footsteps
Mounting the stair, and the door opened. It was his young wife
   Arab, a girl so blonde that her hair
Shone like another lamp at the end of the room, in the dark
   doorway. She stood a moment,
And came quietly and kissed him. "Won't you come down to
   supper, dearest? I will stay here." "No," he said,
And twitched his thumb toward the dark door: she patiently
Went out and closed it.
                        Hungerfield was waiting for his enemy,
And coiled to strike. The conscious upper layer of his mind did
   not one moment believe

That Death had a throat and one could reach it, but his blood
did. What he had seen he had seen. It was dangerous
For any person to come into the room: he had only by force
and will kept his hands
From his dear Arab.

                Meanwhile the gentle click of the door-latch
and Arab's entrance
Had touched the ears of the old woman dying; and slowly, from
nerve-complex to nerve-complex,
Through the oxygen-starved brain crawled into her mind. She
rolled her head on the pillow: "Who is that? There!
There!"
Her tremulous finger pointing at shapes and shadows in the
room twilight, her terrified eyes peering,
Following phantoms. "Nothing, Mother, nothing: there's no
one. Arab was here,
But she has gone." "I'm dying now," she said. "Can't you see?"
She gasped rapidly awhile and whispered, "Not a nice death: no
air." "You will not die, Mother.
You are going to get well."

              It is a common lie to the dying, and
I too have told it; but Hungerfield—
While his mind lied his blood and body believed. He had seen
Death and he would see him again.
He was waiting for his enemy.

              Night deepened around the house;
the sea-waves came up into the stream,
And the stream fought them; the cliffs and standing rocks black
and bone-still
Stood in the dark. There were no stars, there were some little
sparkles of glowworms on the wet ground,

If you looked closely, and shapes of things, and the shifting
   foamline. The vast phantasmagoria of night
Proceeded around that central throat begging for breath, and
   Hungerfield
Sat beside it, rigid and motionless as the rocks but his fingers
   twitching, hunched like a cat
To spring and tear.
                    Then the throat clicked and ceased.
        Hungerfield looked at it; when he looked back
The monster was in the room. It was a column of heavy
   darkness in the dim lamplight, but the arrogant head
Was clear to see. That damned sneer on his face. Hungerfield
   felt his hair rise like a dog's
And heard Death saying scornfully: "Quiet yourself, poor man,
   make no disturbance; it is not for you.
I have come for the old woman Alcmena Hungerfield, to whom
   death
Will be more kind than life." Hungerfield saw his throat and
   sprang at it. But he was like a man swimming
A lake of corpses, the newly harvested souls from all earth's
   fields, faint shrieks and whispers, Death's company.
He smote their dim heads with his hands and their bowels with
   his feet
And swam on them. He reached Death's monstrous flesh and
   they cleared away. It had looked like a shadow,
It was harder than iron. The throat was missed, they stood and
   hugged each other like lovers; Hungerfield
Drove his knee to the groin. Death laughed and said,
"I am not a man," and the awful embrace tightened
On the man's loins; he began to be bent backward, writhing
   and sobbing; he felt the years of his age

Bite at his heart like rats: he was not yet fifty: but it is known
  that little by little God abandons men
When thirty's past. Experience and cunning may perhaps
  increase
But power departs. He struck short at the throat and was bent
  further backward, and suddenly
Flung himself back and fell, dragging Death down with him,
  twisting in the fall, and weasel-quick on the floor
Tore at the throat: then the horrible stench and hopelessness of
  dead bodies filled the dim air; he thought
He had wounded Death. What? The iron force and frame of
  nature with his naked hands? It bubbled and gasped,
"You fool—what have you done!" The iron flesh in his grip
  melted like a summer corpse, and turning liquid
Slid from his hands. He stood up foaming and groped for it;
  there was nothing. He saw in the stair-door
Arab, and Ross his brother, and the hired cattlehand
Staring with eyes like moons. They had heard a chair crash and
  seen the fury; Arab had screamed like a hawk,
But no one heard her; now she stood moaning, gazing at him.
  But Ross entered the room and walked
Carefully wide around him to their mother's bed. The old
  woman was sitting up and breathed easily, saying
"I saw it all. Listen: they are taking him away." A strain of
  mournful music was heard, from the house
Flitting up the black night. This was the time—it was near
  midnight here—for a quarter of an hour
Nobody died. Disease went on, and the little peripheral
  prophetic wars, the famines and betrayals,
Neither man nor beast died, though they might cry for him.

Death, whom we hate and love, had met a worse monster
And could not come.

Hungerfield writhed his mouth, striving to
speak, and failed. He stood swaying,
And spoke loud but not clearly: "To kill the swine. How did he
get—" He lurched a step toward the bed
And righted the fallen chair and sat on it, vulture-hunched and
gray-faced. Then Arab ran to him,
But stopped a man's length distant: "Dear, are you hurt?"
"No," he said. "Keep away from me." "Oh God, I'm in
terror of you.
What have you done?" "Nothing. Nothing at all. I wiped the
damned sneer off his face but he got away from me."
She, with her hands on her throat, like a leaf shaking:
"Who was it, who?" "Uh," he said. "Death. Can't you smell
him? But the swine tricked me,
And slip-slopped out." He worked his hard hands and stared at
them: "Ross, is there any liquor in the house?"
"Drunkard,"
The old woman answered, "as your father was." "Yea?" he said.
"You're better, uh?
You'll be all right, Mother."

In the morning she dressed herself
without help, in the dim of dawn,
And came downstairs. Then Hungerfield, who had watched all
night beside her and dozed in the graying, awoke
And followed down. He made a fire in the stove, and washed
his hands and sliced meat; the old woman fried it
And brought the coffee to boil. Arab came in with her little
son, who ran to Hungerfield:

"What happened, Daddy?" "Your grandmother has got well,"
    he answered. "Then why is Mahmie so scared?" "Uh? No.
Your Mahmie's glad.—Arab," he said, "I know there's a little
    whiskey hidden in the house.
By God I want it." She smiled, and brought a half bottle from
    the linen-closet behind the linen. He said
To his mother, "Don't look, Mother," and filled a water-glass
    full and drained it; she watched him with sidelong hatred
Through her gray brows. "Take a little more," she said, "and go
    blind—
While Ross goes in to Arab and Death to me." "I had my
    hands in him," he said—"Uh?—What?
What did you say?" "I said that one of my two sons is a
    drunken bully, and the other defiles
His brother's wife." He stared at her and said, "You're . . .
    pretty sick, Mother. Forget it, Arab.
Something has happened to her." "Something has happened to
    me," the old woman answered. "I was dying and you filled
    the room
With beastly violence. My beautiful dark angel, my lord and
    love, who like a bridegroom had come for me,
You took him by the throat and killed him. Will you like it,
    Arab,
When he kills Ross?" The girl suddenly knelt to her, where she
    was sitting, and laid her hands on her knees:
"Please tell the truth, Mother." "I'm telling the truth. From my
    windows I watched you. He will surely kill him,
He kills horses and men."

                    Ross at that moment sleepily came in
    the room. The old woman said,

"How do you dare?" "What?" he said. "How do you dare to
   come in, where our handy killer whom you dishonored
Waits for your throat?" Then Arab, her face withered half size
   and as white as paper, leaped up from kneeling:
"Quit lying, Mother!" and furiously turned on Hungerfield, who
   had not stirred, "Be quiet!" she said. "Stand still!
It is a dream from hell." "No," he said quietly, "from the
   morphine.
They get delusions." He looked over Arab's head at his brother:
   "It's all right, Ross." And to his mother:
"I have to think you're mistaken." "Tell that sulphur-haired
   harlot," she screamed, pointing, "that I always hated her—
And well she earns it. I watched their antics.
I kept it quiet while I died, not to cause trouble: but you force
   me to live in this horrible world;
I'll see it straight. Here's a knife, Hawl—
If you're tired from last night." Suddenly she hooded her face
   with her hands
And wept in them. "Don't you believe me, Hawl? You are as
   quiet as a great cold stone standing there,
Standing there blind—." "I think you're still sick, Mother. You
   will get well." "What have you done to me?" she answered.
"What awful thing? All that I said was false and I knew it.
You are all good and faithful, so far as I know. I hate life.
I hate the world. O children, pray for me.
Forgive me: I might have managed a horror here—
If your minds had been quick—" "I think you're still troubled
   by the drug, Mother," he answered; and Arab's child
Began to wail like a little dog that has lost his master. He is all
   alone by the bombed house,

And they never come home; he sits in the empty gate, his
     mouth small and rounded, turned straight to heaven,
Starving, and wails.
                  The old woman watched Arab trying to
     quiet him,
And spoke, but no one through the crying of the child
Could hear her words. She tottered up from her chair and
     reached her hands to him, but Arab
Turned her shoulder against her, hugging him from her; then
     little Norrie (they called him) ceased crying,
But only sobbed, and looked up dimly through tears and said
"Granma." She reached her hands to him. "He knows already,
     he knows what life is, it breaks his heart;
But we shall be so good to him . . . O little pearl, little wet
     frightened face, flower in the rain,
Forgive me, dear, I forgot
That I have someone to live for and love and pray for. Come to
     me, dear." Hungerfield watched her carefully,
And said, "Let her have him, Arab." "No," she said, "I will
     not." His eyes darkened toward wrath. The old woman
     said,
"You know that I'd never hurt him. Are you jealous of me? Will
     you come to Granma, dearest?" He smiled at her
Over Arab's arm. "See now, he's not afraid of me—" "*I* am
     afraid of you," Arab answered,
And took the child in her arms out of the room.
                        All that day
The old woman wandered about the house unreconciled,
     wringing her hands, peering at the household things,

Jealous of changes. Hungerfield remained near her, fearing that
    his great enemy might yet return—
Not hoping now—for his wrath was spent and his blood stilled,
Like the black ebb of the sea, cold, flat and still: deep-lying
    rocks, furred with dark weed and slime,
Rise from the slack. Suddenly she turned on him, crying wildly,
    "Let me alone! You've done enough to me.
D' y' have to follow me like a monstrous poodle all through the
    house?" He patiently answered, "Well, Mother—
You nearly died . . ." "I died," she said, "and you dragged me
    back, to gloat on my misery.
O you are very brave with your strangler hands: your murderous
    hands tearing the holy angel of God—
God will punish you for it." "God-if-there-is-a-God," he
    answered wearily, "is neutral, it is nothing to him.
He has the stars." He made a thin smile on his mouth and said,
    "—as America
Ought to have been." "He is punishing *me*," she said. "I know
    for what crime: life is the crime. I gave you
The horrible gift, I was ignorant and gave it.
I forced out that great head of yours between my thighs,
    bleeding and screaming, tearing myself to pieces:
I am now punished for it—and the monstrous plant that grew
    up out of my body is the stick to beat me:
That's you, that's you!" "You've had a bad time, mother," he
    answered patiently. "You'll soon be better, I think.
Will you go up to town to the doctor with me? Or the young
    doctor
Can come down here." "I had one friend in the world," she
    answered, "loving and faithful: when he came you killed him.

I hate your hangdog face and your horrible hands: I cannot
      bear you: have mercy on me,
Get out of my sight." He felt a sharp gust of wrath returning: "I
      didn't kill him:
By God I *will.*" "I am so homesick for him, his peace and love,
      it is pitiful," she answered.
But she came more into control of herself
As the days passed. She stared at the sea a great deal; she
      watched the sunsets burn fierce and low, or the cormorants
Roosting on the offshore rock, their sharp black wings half
      spread, and black snaky throats; and the restless gulls
Riding the air-streams. She watched coldly the great south
      storms, the tiger-striped, mud-yellow on purple black,
Rage in the offing. She seemed to find consolation in them.
      There is no consolation in humanity—
Though Arab sometimes allowed her (carefully in her presence)
      to hold
Little Norrie in her arms—only the acts and glory of unhuman
      nature or immortal God
Can ever give our hurts peace.
                         But Alcmena Hungerfield
Was not for peace; she had become Death's little dog, stolen
      from him
By the strong hand, yelping all night for her dear master. She
      stared at the sea a great deal, and her son
Came in from Monterey, stinking of whiskey but not altered by
      it. "Here's the paper, Mother,"
He said, and laid it carefully on her knees, the Monterey
      newspaper

With headlines about the outflash of war in Asia. "We've got
　　our nose caught in the door again.
We always do." "Well . . . what?" she answered, staring at him
As she stared at the sea. "I thought you might be int'rested,"
　　he answered. "Ross and I are too old
To go to it." She turned to an inner page and read,
Squinting her eyes to pull the print into shape, in the manner
　　of old age
In lack of glasses. Suddenly she began to tremble and said,
　　"Thank God!
Why did you lie to me, Hawl? People still die." "So do the
　　calves," he answered,
"Three or four every night, and no reason known." "Why did
　　you lie about it then? Look here—"
She thrust the paper at him, trembling and pointing—"Satella
　　Venner died yesterday, my old friend.
I never liked the old woman, but I'd like to go." "Uh," he said,
　　"the funeral? Sure.
I'll take you there." "I want to see her dead face," she
　　answered.

In the night Arab sat up,
Gasping with fear. "Wake up!" she whispered. He lay inert,
　　softly breathing; she dug her finger-ends
Into his great shoulder and the softer flesh over the gullet:
　　"Wake up for God's sake, Hawl.
He has come in!" Hungerfield brushed the little hand from his
　　throat like a biting fly and said
Quietly, "What?" "Something came in," she whispered through
　　clicking teeth. "I can hear it padding

Inside the house." "All hell," he said impatiently; but slid from
    bed and went about the house naked,
Flashing the little electric torch into doors and corners, for the
    night was black. He went upstairs
To the loft where his mother lay, and heard her on the bed
    quietly breathing. He drew the torchlight across,
And her eyes were wide open. "Are you all right, Mother? It's
    Hawl." She made no answer. He stood awhile,
And said, "Good night, Mother." He went back to bed, and
    Arab
Sat huddled on it, small as a frightened child, hugging her
    knees to her throat. "Every night I hear it
Hulking around the house, pawing at the walls—
But tonight it came in." "Lie down," he said, "and be quiet."
    "Let her die, Hawl, she is so unhappy.
O let her die!" "Little fool," he said, "there was nobody. I'm
    sorry for her. Unhappy—what's that?
We win or *they* do." "I pray you, Hawl," she answered, "as if
    you were God: when *my* time comes
O let me die!"

                                In the morning Hungerfield took his mother to
    Monterey, to her friend's funeral. They drove home
Late in the afternoon in the amber afterglow. The day had been
    like a festival. Hungerfield
Accepted his mother's mood and was patient with her, and had
    supper with her
On the Monterey fish-pier, they alone together. He thought that
    she seemed at last perhaps
Not quite unhappy. She was even willing to taste wine, in the
    bright wind on the platform

Over the gentle sea, and made no objection to him
That what he drank was more violent than wine. She had even
    urged him to it, saying that the day
Was a holiday; he failed to observe the calculation
In her old eyes.
                    They were driving the coast-road
Where it loops into Torres Canyon over great precipices in the
    heavy half-light. She said, "De Angulo
Went down here, he lay all night in the butt of the gorge,
    broken to bits, but conscious,
Lying crushed on his dead son, under the engine of the
    car—let's try, let's try!"—she leaped at the steering wheel,
Trying to slew it to the right, to the blue chasm: it was firm as
    rock. She like a mountain-cat
Fought with her fingernails her son's hands; he said indulgently,
    "Don't be afraid, Mother. *I'm* driving.
You are quite safe." "Safe in hell," she panted. "Oh—child—
What have I done to your hands!" They rounded the great
    headlands and came to Granite Point and drove down
Into the heavy fog clotted on Horse Creek.
                              The front of the house
    was empty and blind
When they came near; only at the side two dim-lit rectangles
Faintly reddened the fog-stream. The front door stood wide
    open; the steps were wet. Hungerfield
Helped his mother out of the car and they climbed them. A
    wavering light
Walked in the room: Ross came slow to the door, the
    smoke-blackened glass lamp skew in his hand;
He moved a chair with the other and said,

"Sit down, Mother," "We've had supper," she said. "I'll go
straight to bed." Hungerfield said fiercely:
"What's the matter? Where's Arab?" "Gone . . . gone," he
answered. His face was like a skull, stripped and hollow,
and the lamp
Rolled in his hand, so that his brother took it and said,
"Are you drunk, Ross?" He mumbled, "Unq-uh," shaking his
head. "Four more calves and your bay horse
Are—*dead*—" he screamed the word—"He comes behind you,
Hawl,
He works 'n the dark"—his head still shaking, apparently he
could not stop it; his hair and his shirt hung
As if they were soaked with water. Hungerfield said, "You fool:
talk sense.
Where has she gone?" "Oh, wait," he said, "for God's sake,"
pointing at the inner doorway; and gulped and shivered:
"In there." Hungerfield set the lamp down and strode to the
door: it was pitch dark within: he said, "Arab?
Are you there, Arab?" Ross echoed him for no reason, saying
loudly,
"Arab." His brother entered the room and they heard him
fumbling in it, and his voice: "Where are you?" The old
woman,
Leaning against the chair-back, said coolly: "Well, Ross,
What has happened?" "Mother," he said. He stood moving his
lips without further words, and they heard Hungerfield
Move blind in the black room, and croak
In a strange voice, "Light, light!" They stood and stared at each
other; then Ross opened his mouth and sucked

His lungs full, as if he were going to dive into deep water; he
     took the lamp from the table and carried it
To the dark room. The old woman followed him; and in the
     room quickly found matches, and lighted
A second lamp.
               Arab and little Norrie lay without life together
     on the narrow bed,
Phantoms of what they had been. Hungerfield stood above
     them, gaunt, straight and staring
At Arab's discolored hair: their clothes and their yellow hair
     soaked with water and foam. Hungerfield said,
"I knew in the dark well enough." A frond of sea-weed stuck
     beside the child's nostrils, but Arab's face
Was clean pale marble; except her eyes were open, blue and
     suffused, and her half open mouth
Had foam inside. Hungerfield said heavily, "How did they
     drown?" Ross answered:
"I dived and pulled them out. I pumped her ribs with my hands
     for an hour, I think,
And she grew cold." Hungerfield heavily turned and said:
"Why did they go in water?" Ross answered, "He comes behind
     you, you know. I heard her screaming—" The old woman
Went around the bed and dropped by the child, her knees loud
     on the floor, her shaking gray head
On the child's breast. Ross said, "I was at the stable, you know,
     unsaddling. I ran down and saw her
Running out on the rocks carrying the baby, crying and
     running. She thought someone was after her.
She either jumped or fell in." "So that's your help,"
     Hungerfield said. He felt his arm swell and strike—

One blow, but the neck broke. They heard the head strike the
    floor and the body shuddering, and Hungerfield
Did not look down. The old woman lifted up her desert-dry
    eyes from the child's breast and said:
"You've done it now." He stood considering the matter, hearing
    the rub of Ross's boots on the floor
As he twitched and was dying. "Ah," Hungerfield said, "I did
    it. Yes. My monstrous fault." "Oh," she answered,
"Now me, now me!" "The fool had to interfere," he answered.
    He knuckled his eyes and said heavily,
"I have another son in Alaska. I have no other brother and no
    other love. Arab.
Arab alone." You've had many," she answered eagerly. "Look,"
    he said,
"Oh, she was beautiful, Mother. She was always sweet, patient,
    and cheerful; she loved Norrie—and now
She has death in her mouth."

                            As if his name had called him, Death
Stood in the room. Alcmena Hungerfield well remembered him,
The towering stature, the high thick shoulders and the
    arrogance, the long dark narrow face and deep eyes
Set close together. "O dear dark God," she said, "I am here.
    Gently I pray." But Hungerfield
Gazing at Arab's face did not hear her, and did not see
What came behind him and with a slight motion of the hand
    beckoned
To Ross to come. The old woman saw the unfleshed soul
Blind and erratic as a beetle flying rise from the body; it jigged
    and darted in the air, and swam

Into Death's hand, which crushed it. Hungerfield turned and
 said, "Is it you, Horse-face? I haven't called you yet.
Come again in ten minutes." He turned away, saying, "Arab is
 dead. My dear Arab is dead.
And Ross, who was quick and loyal, skillful with cattle and a
 great rider, is dead. My brave little man
Norrie is dead. —Hell, he gets three for one, and now the
 whole game, he has tricked me witless.
But I'll make a good sunset—We'll dance in fire, Horse-face,
And go up yelling."
         He went in the dark to
 the kitchen store-room and fetched the big can of coal-oil,
Going heavily like a rock walking, violent and certain; but in
 the darkness returning
He walked into a half open door, and with one hand
Tore it down from the hinges. He poured the coal-oil onto the
 floor and the bed and the wooden walls,
And turned a lamp to flaring and flung it
Into the oil-pool. Bright flame stood up. The old woman said,
 "Hawl . . .
Kill me before I burn." He said, "I've done enough and too
 much, Mother.
Find a knife for yourself." She, thinly laughing: "You're not
 much help, are you? But I've lived with pain
As fish live with the sea. Or if it's tough I can drink smoke."
 But her courage after a time
Failed, and she fled from the house before the bright flame
 embraced her.

Horse Creek sea-mouth at last for once
Was full of light; the fire drove away the fog; there was light
    everywhere. Black rock shone bright as blood;
The stream and the deep-throated waves of the ocean glittered
    with crimson lightnings, and the low cloud
Gaped like a lion's mouth, swallowing the flights of flame and
    the soul of a man. It is thus (and will be) that violence
Turns on itself, and builds on the wreck of violence its violent
    beauty, the spring fire-fountain
And final peace: grim in the desert in the lion's carcass the hive
    of honey. But Alcmena Hungerfield
Hating both life and death fled from the place. She lived two
    years yet, Death remembering her son, and died
As others do.

            Here is the poem, dearest; you will never read it
    nor hear it. You were more beautiful
Than a hawk flying; you were faithful and a lion heart like this
    rough hero Hungerfield. But the ashes have fallen
And the flame has gone up; nothing human remains. You are
    earth and air; you are in the beauty of the ocean
And the great streaming triumphs of sundown; you are alive
    and well in the tender young grass rejoicing
When soft rain falls all night, and little rosy-fleeced clouds float
    on the dawn. —I shall be with you presently.

DE RERUM VIRTUTE

I

Here is the skull of a man: a man's thoughts and emotions
Have moved under the thin bone vault like clouds
Under the blue one: love and desire and pain,
Thunderclouds of wrath and white gales of fear
Have hung inside here: and sometimes the curious desire of
    knowing
Values and purpose and the causes of things
Has coasted like a little observer airplane over the images
That filled this mind: it never discovered much,
And now all's empty, a bone bubble, a blown-out eggshell.

II

That's what it's like: for the egg too has a mind,
Doing what our able chemists will never do,
Building the body of a hatchling, choosing among the proteins:
These for the young wing-muscles, these for the great
Crystalline eyes, these for the flighty nerves and brain:
Choosing and forming: a limited but superhuman intelligence,
Prophetic of the future and aware of the past:
The hawk's egg will make a hawk, and the serpent's
A gliding serpent: but each with a little difference
From its ancestors—and slowly, if it works, the race
Forms a new race: that also is a part of the plan
Within the egg. I believe the first living cell
Had echoes of the future in it, and felt
Direction and the great animals, the deep green forest

And whale's-track sea; I believe this globed earth
Not all by chance and fortune brings forth her broods,
But feels and chooses. And the Galaxy, the firewheel
On which we are pinned, the whirlwind of stars in which our
sun is one dust-grain, one electron, this giant atom of the
universe
Is not blind force, but fulfills its life and intends its courses.
"All things are full of God.
Winter and summer, day and night, war and peace are God."
III
Thus the thing stands; the labor and the games go on—
What for? What for? —Am I a god that I should know?
Men live in peace and happiness; men live in horror
And die howling. Do you think the blithe sun
Is ignorant that black waste and beggarly blindness trail him like
hounds,
And will have him at last? He will be strangled
Among his dead satellites, remembering magnificence.
IV
I stand on the cliff at Sovranes creek-mouth.
Westward beyond the raging water and the bent shoulder of the
world
The bitter futile war in Korea proceeds, like an idiot
Prophesying. It is too hot in mind
For anyone, except God perhaps, to see beauty in it. Indeed it
is hard to see beauty
In any of the acts of man: but that means the acts of a sick
microbe
On a satellite of a dust-grain twirled in a whirlwind
In the world of stars. . . .

Something perhaps may come of him; in any event
He can't last long.—Well: I am short of patience
Since my wife died . . . and this era of spite and hate-filled
    half-worlds
Gets to the bone. I believe that man too is beautiful,
But it is hard to see, and wrapped up in falsehoods.
    Michelangelo and the Greek sculptors—
How they flattered the race! Homer and Shakespeare—
How they flattered the race!

v

One light is left us: the beauty of things, not men;
The immense beauty of the world, not the human world.
Look—and without imagination, desire nor dream—directly
At the mountains and sea. Are they not beautiful?
These plunging promontories and flame-shaped peaks
Stopping the somber stupendous glory, the storm-fed ocean?
                    Look at the Lobos Rocks off the shore,
With foam flying at their flanks, and the long sea-lions
Couching on them. Look at the gulls on the cliff-wind,
And the soaring hawk under the cloud-stream—
But in the sagebrush desert, all one sun-stricken
Color of dust, or in the reeking tropical rain-forest,
Or in the intolerant north and high thrones of ice—is the earth
    not beautiful?
Nor the great skies over the earth?
The beauty of things means virtue and value in them.
It is in the beholder's eye, not the world? Certainly.
It is the human mind's translation of the transhuman
Intrinsic glory. It means that the world is sound,
Whatever the sick microbe does. But he too is part of it.

CARMEL POINT

The extraordinary patience of things!
This beautiful place defaced with a crop of suburban houses—
How beautiful when we first beheld it,
Unbroken field of poppy and lupin walled with clean cliffs;
No intrusion but two or three horses pasturing,
Or a few milch cows rubbing their flanks on the outcrop
    rockheads—
Now the spoiler has come: does it care?
Not faintly. It has all time. It knows the people are a tide
That swells and in time will ebb, and all
Their works dissolve. Meanwhile the image of the pristine
    beauty
Lives in the very grain of the granite,
Safe as the endless ocean that climbs our cliff.—As for us:
We must uncenter our minds from ourselves;
We must unhumanize our views a little, and become confident
As the rock and ocean that we were made from.

 SKUNKS

The corruptions of war and peace, the public and wholesale
        crimes that make war, the greed and lies of the peace
And victor's vengeance: how at a distance
They soften into romance—blue mountains and blossomed
        marshes in the long landscape of history—Caligula
Becomes an amusing clown, and Genghiz
A mere genius, a great author of tragedies. Our own time's
        chiefs of massacre—Stalin died yesterday—
Watch how soon blood will bleach, and gross horror
Become words in a book.
                                We have little animals here,
        slow-stepping cousins of stoat and weasel,
Striped skunks, that can spit from under their tails
An odor so vile and stifling that neither wolf nor wildcat dares
        to come near them; they walk in confidence,
Solely armed with this loathsome poison-gas.
But smelled far off—have you noticed?—it is surprisingly
        pleasant.
                                It is like the breath of ferns and wet earth
Deep in a wooded glen in the evening,
Cool water glides quietly over the moss-grown stones, quick
        trout dimple the pool.—Distance makes clean.

ANIMALS

At dawn a knot of sea-lions lies off the shore
In the slow swell between the rock and the cliff,
Sharp flippers lifted, or great-eyed heads, as they roll in the sea,
Bigger than draft-horses, and barking like dogs
Their all-night song. It makes me wonder a little
That life near kin to human, intelligent, hot-blooded, idle and
      singing, can float at ease
In the ice-cold midwinter water. Then, yellow dawn
Colors the south, I think about the rapid and furious lives in
      the sun:
They have little to do with ours; they have nothing to do with
      oxygen and salted water; they would look monstrous
If we could see them: the beautiful passionate bodies of living
      flame, batlike flapping and screaming,
Tortured with burning lust and acute awareness, that ride the
      storm-tides
Of the great fire-globe. They are animals, as we are. There are
      many other chemistries of animal life
Besides the slow oxidation of carbohydrates and amino-acids.

THE DEER LAY DOWN THEIR BONES

I followed the narrow cliffside trail half way up the mountain
Above the deep river-canyon. There was a little cataract crossed
the path, flinging itself
Over tree roots and rocks, shaking the jeweled fern-fronds,
bright bubbling water
Pure from the mountain, but a bad smell came up. Wondering
at it I clambered down the steep stream
Some forty feet, and found in the midst of bush-oak and laurel,
Hung like a bird's nest on the precipice brink a small hidden
clearing,
Grass and a shallow pool. But all about there were bones lying
in the grass, clean bones and stinking bones,
Antlers and bones: I understood that the place was a refuge for
wounded deer; there are so many
Hurt ones escape the hunters and limp away to lie hidden; here
they have water for the awful thirst
And peace to die in; dense green laurel and grim cliff
Make sanctuary, and a sweet wind blows upward from the deep
gorge.—I wish my bones were with theirs.
But that's a foolish thing to confess, and a little cowardly. We
know that life
Is on the whole quite equally good and bad, mostly gray neutral,
and can be endured
To the dim end, no matter what magic of grass, water and
precipice, and pain of wounds,
Makes death look dear. We have been given life and have used
it—not a great gift perhaps—but in honesty

Should use it all. Mine's empty since my love died—Empty? The
  flame-haired grandchild with great blue eyes
That look like hers?—What can I do for the child? I gaze at her
  and wonder what sort of man
In the fall of the world . . . I am growing old, that is the
  trouble. My children and little grandchildren
Will find their way, and why should I wait ten years yet, having
  lived sixty-seven, ten years more or less,
Before I crawl out on a ledge of rock and die snapping, like a
  wolf
Who has lost his mate?—I am bound by my own thirty-year-old
  decision: who drinks the wine
Should take the dregs; even in the bitter lees and sediment
New discovery may lie. The deer in that beautiful place lay
  down their bones: I must wear mine.

The unformed volcanic earth, a female thing,
Furiously following with the other planets
Their lord the sun: her body is molten metal pressed rigid
By its own mass; her beautiful skin, basalt and granite and the
    lighter elements,
Swam to the top. She was like a mare in her heat eyeing the
    stallion,
Screaming for life in the womb; her atmosphere
Was the breath of her passion: not the blithe air
Men breathe and live, but marsh-gas, ammonia, sulphured
    hydrogen,
Such poison as our remembering bodies return to
When they die and decay and the end of life
Meets its beginning. The sun heard her and stirred
Her thick air with fierce lightnings and flagellations
Of germinal power, building impossible molecules, amino-acids
And flashy unstable proteins: thence life was born,
Its nitrogen from ammonia, carbon from methane,
Water from the cloud and salts from the young seas,
It dribbled down into the primal ocean like a babe's urine
Soaking the cloth: heavily built protein molecules
Chemically growing, bursting apart as the tensions
In the inordinate molecule become unbearable—
That is to say, growing and reproducing themselves, a virus
On the warm ocean.
             Time and the world changed,
The proteins were no longer created, the ammoniac atmosphere

And the great storms no more. This virus now
Must labor to maintain itself. It clung together
Into bundles of life, which we call cells,
With microscopic walls enclosing themselves
Against the world. But why would life maintain itself,
Being nothing but a dirty scum on the sea
Dropped from foul air? Could it perhaps perceive
Glories to come? Could it foresee that cellular life
Would make the mountain forest and the eagle dawning,
Monstrously beautiful, wings, eyes and claws, dawning
Over the rock-ridge? And the passionate human intelligence
Straining its limits, striving to understand itself and the universe
      to the last galaxy—
Flammantia moenia mundi, Lucretius wrote,
Alliterating like a Saxon—all those Ms mean majesty—
The flaming world-walls, far-flung fortifications of being
Against not-being.
               For after a time the cells of life
Bound themselves into clans, a multitude of cells
To make one being—as the molecules before
Had made of many one cell. Meanwhile they had invented
Chlorophyll and ate sunlight, cradled in peace
On the warm waves; but certain assassins among them
Discovered that it was easier to eat flesh
Than feed on lean air and sunlight: thence the animals,
Greedy mouths and guts, life robbing life,
Grew from the plants; and as the ocean ebbed and flowed many
      plants and animals
Were stranded in the great marshes along the shore,
Where many died and some lived. From these grew all land-life,

Plants, beasts and men; the mountain forest and the mind of
Aeschylus
And the mouse in the wall.

What is this thing called life?—But I believe
That the earth and stars too, and the whole glittering universe,
and rocks on the mountain have life,
Only we do not call it so—I speak of the life
That oxydizes fats and proteins and carbo-
Hydrates to live on, and from that chemical energy
Makes pleasure and pain, wonder, love, adoration, hatred and
terror: how do these thing grow
From a chemical reaction?
I think they were here already. I think
the rocks
And the earth and the other planets, and the stars and galaxies
Have their various consciousness, all things are conscious;
But the nerves of an animal, the nerves and brain
Bring it to focus; the nerves and brain are like a burning-glass
To concentrate the heat and make it catch fire:
It seems to us martyrs hotter than the blazing hearth
From which it came. So we scream and laugh, clamorous
animals
Born howling to die groaning: the old stones in the dooryard
Prefer silence: but those and all things have their own
awareness,
As the cells of a man have; they feel and feed and influence
each other, each unto all,
Like the cells of a man's body making one being,
They make one being, one consciousness, one life, one God.

But whence came the race of man? I will make a guess.

A change of climate killed the great northern forests,

Forcing the manlike apes down from their trees,

They starved up there. They had been secure up there,

But famine is no security: among the withered branches blue
  famine:

They had to go down to the earth, where green still grew

And small meats might be gleaned. But there the great
  flesh-eaters,

Tiger and panther and the horrible fumbling bear and endless
  wolf-packs made life

A dream of death. Therefore man has these dreams,

And kills out of pure terror. Therefore man walks erect,

Forever alerted: as the bear rises to fight

So man does always. Therefore he invented fire and flint
  weapons

In his desperate need. Therefore he is cruel and bloody-handed
  and quick-witted, having survived

Against all odds. Never blame the man: his hard-pressed

Ancestors formed him: the other anthropoid apes were safe

In the great southern rain-forest and hardly changed

In a million years: but the race of man was made

By shock and agony. Therefore they invented the song called
  language

To celebrate their survival and record their deeds. And
  therefore the deeds they celebrate—

Achilles raging in the flame of the south, Baltic Beowulf like a
  fog-blinded sea-bear

Prowling the blasted fenland in the bleak twilight to the black
  water—

Are cruel and bloody. Epic, drama and history,
Jesus and Judas, Jenghiz, Julius Caesar, no great poem
Without the blood-splash. They are a little lower than the
    angels, as someone said.—Blood-snuffing rats:
But never blame them: a wound was made in the brain
When life became too hard, and has never healed.
It is there that they learned trembling religion and
    blood-sacrifice,
It is there that they learned to butcher beasts and to slaughter
    men,
And hate the world: the great religions of love and kindness
May conceal that, not change it. They are not primary but
    reactions
Against the hate: as the eye after feeding on a red sunfall
Will see green suns.
                The human race is one of God's
    sense-organs,
Immoderately alerted to feel good and evil
And pain and pleasure. It is a nerve-ending,
Like eye, ear, taste-buds (hardly able to endure
The nauseous draught) it is a sensory organ of God's.
As Titan-mooded Lear or Prometheus reveal to their audience
Extremes of pain and passion they will never find
In their own lives but through the poems as sense-organs
They feel and know them: so the exultations and agonies of
    beasts and men
Are sense-organs of God: and on other globes
Throughout the universe much greater nerve-endings
Enrich the consciousness of the one being
Who is all that exists. This is man's mission:

To find and feel; all animal experience
Is a part of God's life. He would be balanced and neutral
As a rock on the shore, but the red sunset-waves
Of life's passions fling over him. He endures them,
We endure ours. That ancient wound in the brain
Has never healed, it hangs wide, it lets in the stars
Into the animal-stinking ghost-ridden darkness, the human soul.
The mind of man. . . .
Slowly, perhaps, man may grow into it—
Do you think so? This villainous king of beasts, this deformed
     ape?—He has mind
And imagination, he might go far
And end in honor. The hawks are more heroic but man has a
     steeper mind,
Huge pits of darkness, high peaks of light,
You may calculate a comet's orbit or the dive of a hawk, not a
     man's mind.

ON AN ANTHOLOGY
OF CHINESE POEMS

Beautiful the hanging cliff and the wind-thrown cedars, but they
　　have no weight.
Beautiful the fantastically
Small farmhouse and ribbon of rice-fields a mile below; and
　　billows of mist
Blow through the gorge. These men were better
Artists than any of ours, and far better observers. They loved
　　landscape
And put man in his place. But why
Do their rocks have no weight? They loved rice-wine and peace
　　and friendship,
Above all they loved landscape and solitude,
—Like Wordsworth. But Wordsworth's mountains have weight
　　and mass, dull though the song be.
It is a moral difference perhaps?

# OYSTERS

On the wide Texan and New Mexican ranches
They call them prairie oysters, but here on the Pacific
    coast-range,
Mountain oysters. The spring round-up was finished,
The calves had been cut and branded and their ears notched,
And staggered with their pain up the mountain. A vast rose
    and gold sunset, very beautiful, made in April,
Moved overhead. The men had gone down to the ranch-house,
But three old men remained by the dying branding-fire
At the corral gate, Lew Clark and Gilchrist
And Onofrio the Indian; they searched the trampled
Earth by the fire, gathering the testicles of gelded bull-calves
Out of the bloody dust; they peeled and toasted them
Over the dying branding-fire and chewed them down,
Grinning at each other, believing that the masculine glands
Would renew youth.

                    The unhappy calves bawled in their pain
        and their mothers answered them.
The vast sunset, all colored, all earnest, all golden withdrew a
    little higher but made a fierce heart
Against the sea-line, spouting a sudden red glare like the eye of
    God. The old men
Chewed at their meat. I do not believe the testicles of
    bull-calves
Will make an old man young again, but if they could—
What fools those old men are. Age brings hard burdens,

But at worst cools hot blood and sets men free
From the sexual compulsions that madden youth.
Why would they dip their aging bodies again
Into that fire? For old men death's the fire,
Let them dream beautiful death, not women's loins.

What ancestor of mine in wet Wales or wild Scotland
Was named Godfrey?—from which by the Anglo-French erosion
Geoffrey, Jeffry's son, Jeffries, Jeffers in Ireland—
A totally undistinguished man; the whirlwinds of history
Passed him and passed him by. They marked him no doubt,
Hurt him or helped him, they rolled over his head
And he I suppose fought back, but entirely unnoticed;
Nothing of him remains.

                I should like to meet him,
And sit beside him, drinking his muddy beer,
Talking about the Norman nobles and parish politics
And the damned foreigners: I think his tales of woe
Would be as queer as ours, and even farther
From reality. His mind was as quick as ours
But perhaps even more credulous.

                  He was a Christian
No doubt—I am not dreaming back into prehistory—
And christened Godfrey, which means the peace of God.
He never in his life found it, when he died it found him.
He has been dead six or eight centuries,
Mouldering in some forgotten British graveyard, nettles and
    rain-slime.

Nettlebed: I remember a place in Oxfordshire,
That prickly name, I have twisted and turned on a bed of
    nettles
All my life long: an apt name for life: nettlebed.

Deep under it swim the dead, down the dark tides and bloodshot eras of time, bathed in God's peace.

# CREMATION

It nearly cancels my fear of death, my dearest said,
When I think of cremation. To rot in the earth
Is a loathsome end, but to roar up in flame—besides, I am used
    to it,
I have flamed with love or fury so often in my life,
No wonder my body is tired, no wonder it is dying.
We had great joy of my body. Scatter the ashes.

GRANDDAUGHTER

And here's a portrait of my granddaughter Una
When she was two years old: a remarkable painter,
A perfect likeness; nothing tricky nor modernist,
Nothing of the artist fudging his art into the picture,
But simple and true. She stands in a glade of trees with a still
    inlet
Of blue ocean behind her. Thus exactly she looked then,
A forgotten flower in her hand, those great blue eyes
Asking and wondering.
                  Now she is five years old
And found herself. She does not ask any more but commands,
Sweet and fierce-tempered; that light red hair of hers
Is the fuse for explosions. When she is eighteen
I'll not be here. I hope she will find her natural elements,
Laughter and violence; and in her quiet times
The beauty of things—the beauty of transhuman things,
Without which we are all lost. I hope she will find
Powerful protection and a man like a hawk to cover her.

SALVAGE

It is true that half the glory is gone.
Motors and modernist houses usurp the scene.
There is no eagle soaring, nor a puma
On the Carmel hill highroad, where thirty years ago
We watched one pass. Yet by God's grace
I have still a furlong of granite cliff, on which the Pacific
Leans his wild weight; and the trees I planted
When I was young, little green whips in hand,
Have grown in despite of the biting sea-wind,
And are accepted by nature, an angry-voiced tribe of
     night-herons'
Nests on the boughs. One has to pay for it;
The county taxes take all my income, and it seems ridiculous
To hold three acres of shorelong woodland
And the little low house that my own hands made, at the
     annual cost
Of a shiny new car. Never mind, the trees and the stones are
     worth it.

But it's darker now. I am old, and my wife has died,
Whose eyes made life. As for me, I have to consider and take
     thought
Before I can feel the beautiful secret
In places and stars and stones. To her it came freely.
I wish that all human creatures might feel it.
That would make joy in the world, and make men perhaps a
     little nobler—as a handful of wildflowers.

THE SHEARS

A great dawn-color rose widening the petals around her gold
    eye
Peers day and night in the window. She watches us
Breakfasting, lighting lamps, reading, and the children playing,
    and the dogs by the fire,
She watches earnestly, uncomprehending,
As we stare into the world of trees and roses uncomprehending,
There is a great gulf fixed. But even while
I gaze, and the rose at me, my little flower-greedy
    daughter-in-law
Walks with shears, very blonde and housewifely
Through the small garden, and suddenly the rose finds herself
    rootless in-doors.
Now she is part of the life she watched.
—So we: death comes and plucks us: we become part of the
    living earth
And wind and water whom we so loved. We are they.

VULTURE

I had walked since dawn and lay down to rest on a bare hillside
Above the ocean. I saw through half-shut eyelids a vulture
    wheeling high up in heaven,
And presently it passed again, but lower and nearer, its orbit
    narrowing, I understood then
That I was under inspection. I lay death-still and heard the
    flight-feathers
Whistle above me and make their circle and come nearer.
I could see the naked red head between the great wings
Bear downward staring. I said, "My dear bird, we are wasting
    time here.
These old bones will still work; they are not for you." But how
    beautiful he looked, gliding down
On those great sails; how beautiful he looked, veering away in
    the sea-light over the precipice. I tell you solemnly
That I was sorry to have disappointed him. To be eaten by that
    beak and become part of him, to share those wings and
    those eyes—
What a sublime end of one's body, what an enskyment; what a
    life after death.

BIRDS AND FISHES

Every October millions of little fish come along the shore,
Coasting this granite edge of the continent
On their lawful occasions: but what a festival for the seafowl.
What a witches' sabbath of wings
Hides the dark water. The heavy pelicans shout "Haw!" like
    Job's friend's warhorse
And dive from the high air, the cormorants
Slip their long black bodies under the water and hunt like
    wolves
Through the green half-light. Screaming, the gulls watch,
Wild with envy and malice, cursing and snatching. What
    hysterical greed!
What a filling of pouches! the mob
Hysteria is nearly human—these decent birds!—as if they were
    finding
Gold in the street. It is better than gold,
It can be eaten: and which one in all this fury of wildfowl pities
    the fish?
No one certainly. Justice and mercy
Are human dreams, they do not concern the birds nor the fish
    nor eternal God.
However—look again before you go.
The wings and the wild hungers, the wave-worn skerries, the
    bright quick minnows
Living in terror to die in torment—
Man's fate and theirs—and the island rocks and immense ocean
    beyond, and Lobos

Darkening above the bay: they are beautiful?

That is their quality: not mercy, not mind, not goodness, but
the beauty of God.